Winner of the 2014 Gwen Pharis Ringwood Award for Drama
Winner of the 2013 Betty Mitchell Award for Outstanding New Play
Winner of the 2013/2014 Woodward/Newman Drama Award
Winner of the 2013 Calgary Theatre Critics Award for Best New Script
Winner of the 2011 Grand Prize in the Alberta Playwriting Competition
Finalist for the 2012 STAGE International Script Competition
Longlisted for the 2014 James Tait Black Prize for Drama

"*Sequence* balances smart and heart."
—Stephen Hunt, *Calgary Herald*

"Absolutely one of the most dynamic and intriguing shows I've seen
this year.... *Sequence* doesn't underestimate the audience's ability to
intelligently engage with the notion of luck and coincidence... This
play challenges the audience with smart dialogue about complex
ideas... The entertaining results will give you much to think and talk
about long after the play is done... It will be one of the most interesting and well-conceived shows you've had the pleasure of seeing."
—Jessica Goldman, CBC Radio

"Witty, intelligent, and remarkably funny."
—Doris Lynch, *Bloomington Herald-Times*

"An intellectual Rubik cube that challenges us to consider some
of our most profound questions in a search for some kind of
alignment."
—Colin MacLean, *Edmonton Sun*

"Lakra's script is elegantly written and refuses to spoon feed the
audience."
—Mel Priestley, *Vue Weekly*

# Sequence
by Arun Lakra

**Playwrights Canada Press**
Toronto

For professional or amateur production rights, please contact:
Michael Petrasek at The Talent House
204A St. George Street, Toronto, ON M5R 2N5
416.960.9686, michael@talenthouse.ca

LIBRARY AND ARCHIVES CANADA CATALOGUING IN PUBLICATION
Lakra, Arun, 1966-, author
        Sequence / Arun Lakra.

A play.
Issued in print and electronic formats.
ISBN 978-1-77091-197-0 (pbk.).--ISBN 978-1-77091-198-7 (pdf).--
ISBN 978-1-77091-199-4 (epub)

        I. Title.

PS8623.A4246S46 2014            C812'.6            C2013-908487-8
                                                   C2013-908488-6

We acknowledge the financial support of the Canada Council for the Arts, the Ontario Arts Council (OAC)—an agency of the Government of Ontario, which last year funded 1,681 individual artists and 1,125 organizations in 216 communities across Ontario for a total of $52.8 million—the Ontario Media Development Corporation, and the Government of Canada through the Canada Book Fund for our publishing activities.

Canada Council Conseil des arts
for the Arts     du Canada

ONTARIO ARTS COUNCIL
CONSEIL DES ARTS DE L'ONTARIO
50 YEARS OF ONTARIO GOVERNMENT SUPPORT OF THE ARTS
50 ANS DE SOUTIEN DU GOUVERNEMENT DE L'ONTARIO AUX ARTS

Canada

Ontario
Ontario Media Development
Corporation

to Mom and Dad
for your nature and your nurture

## Author's Notes

The play runs continuously.

For most of the play, the set doubles as a genetics laboratory and an auditorium stage.

When viewed from the audience, the design might loosely resemble a spiral of DNA.

A whiteboard (or chalkboard) extends the entire length of the stage.

Early in the performance, the board is erased. From that point on, the characters illustrate their dialogue using a marker (or chalk). No further erasing is done.

The board may be used to illustrate any dialogue. In the script, specific drawings are identified that may be used to execute a particular staging concept (outlined in the end notes).

Each character may seem to observe the drawings of the others.

Props may be shared by characters from different times and places.

There may be intersections or *wormholes* where the pronunciation, delivery, actions, mannerisms, or physical attributes of Dr. Guzman may be reminiscent of Cynthia's. A similar relationship exists between Theo and Mr. Adamson. For example, Cynthia and Dr. Guzman may use the British pronunciation of the word *laboratory*. Specific light and/or sound cues may be utilized to highlight these intersections.

The transitions between scenes should be seamless and without pause, as if a character's first words in a new scene are a direct response to the last phrase in the previous scene.

Pace is critical. For most of the play, especially during the science-intensive dialogue, there should be a quick and urgent rhythm. These are fast-thinking, fast-talking characters who speak with almost overlapping dialogue. The play lives best at a running time of *not more than eighty minutes*.

*Sequence* received its first workshop through the Alberta Playwrights' Network in 2011. Following this, as part of the award for winning the grand prize in the Alberta Playwriting Competition, *Sequence* received a workshop and a public reading during Theatre Alberta/ Alberta Playwrights' Network's 2011 PlayWorks Ink Conference. *Sequence* was developed further through a special workshop presentation at the 2013 Telluride Playwrights Festival. The play received its world premiere at the Big Secret Theatre in the EPCOR Centre for the Performing Arts, Calgary, Alberta, in a joint production by Downstage and Hit & Myth Productions from February 20 through March 2, 2013. It featured the following cast and creative team:

Theo: Joel Cochrane
Dr. Guzman: Karen Johnson-Diamond
Cynthia: Alana Hawley
Mr. Adamson: Braden Griffiths

Producers: Simon Mallett, Joel Cochrane, and Ellen Close
Director: Kevin McKendrick
Assistant director: Michelle Kneale
Set and co-production designer: Terry Gunvordahl
Lighting and co-production designer: Anton de Groot
Sound designer: Peter Moller
Costume designer: Laura Lottes
Stage manager: Kelsey ter Kuile
Production manager: Tuled Giovanazzi
Production intern: Taryn Haley

*Sequence* received its US premiere in a production by the Bloomington Playwrights Project from October 4 through October 12, 2013, in Bloomington, Indiana. It featured the following cast and creative team:

Theo: Henry A. McDaniel III
Dr. Guzman: Catharine Du Bois
Cynthia: Lauren Sagendorph
Mr. Adamson: Paul Kühne

Producing artistic director: Chad Rabinovitz
Director: Lee Cromwell
Scenic design: David Wade
Lighting design: Tilman Piedmont
Sound design: Brian Donnelly
Costume design: Chib Gratz
Stage manager: Travis Staley

*God does not play dice.*
—Albert Einstein

*The lot is cast into the lap, but its every decision is from the Lord.*
—Proverbs 16:33

*It is possible for the way the universe began to be determined by the laws of science. In that case, it would not be necessary to appeal to God to decide how the universe began. This doesn't prove that there is no God, only that God is not necessary.*
—Stephen Hawking

# Characters

Dr. Guzman: Female. Fifties.
Theo: Male. Fifties.
Mr. Adamson: Male. Twenties.
Cynthia: Female. Twenties.

*Lights up.*

*DR. GUZMAN and THEO enter. THEO carries an unopened umbrella.*

*They converge at the whiteboard. It shows a mess of diagrams, numbers, and words.*

*DR. GUZMAN turns to face the board. She finds an eraser, wipes the board clean.*

*THEO turns to face the audience. With mock trepidation, he pops open the umbrella.*

*Playfully, he peers out from under it, looks upward. He closes the umbrella.*

*THEO moves to the ladder. He circles it. Mysteriously. Mischievously.*

*DR. GUZMAN takes a moment to find a marker. She accidentally drops it, picks it up again.*

*Abruptly, THEO ducks under the ladder. He emerges, welcomes the applause.*

*Chest pain! Is he having a heart attack? No, he's just joking around.*

*DR. GUZMAN writes on the board with her left hand: WHICH CAME FIRST?*

*THEO strides to a wall mirror. He stumbles, almost trips on the way.*

*DR. GUZMAN addresses the audience.*

*THEO fixes his hair in the mirror.*

DR. GUZMAN     The question is, which came first?

*THEO suddenly takes a big swing with his umbrella handle, smashing the mirror.*

The chicken or the egg?

THEO     Macbeth!

*THEO looks up to the heavens, opens his arms, waits for the lightning bolt that never comes.*

DR. GUZMAN     I submit to you, despite popular misconception, that the question is not rhetorical.

*THEO addresses the audience.*

THEO        Luck is like irony. Not everybody who thinks they got it, got it.

DR. GUZMAN        One had to come first. Wouldn't you agree? Unless you postulate *simultaneous* creation. That is, unless you postulate God.

*DR. GUZMAN writes on the board: GOD.*

THEO        Luck is like breasts. It's relative. If everybody had big breasts, we'd just call them breasts. And we wouldn't stare. As much.

*He picks up a marker. He writes on the board: LUCK.*

DR. GUZMAN        But we're scientists, are we not? At least until your final exam results are posted. And we know Borel's Law states if the odds of an event are less than one in ten to the fiftieth, that event will never happen in the entire time and space of our known universe.

THEO        You are not all lucky; I'm sorry to have to break it to you. In fact, I suspect the truly lucky ones are those whose wives did not drag them to a book reading three hours before kickoff on Super Bowl Sunday.

DR. GUZMAN        So the chances of the chicken and the egg evolving simultaneously are perilously close to zero. *Ergo*, it must have been sequential.

THEO        Take a guy in a wheelchair, who can't even take a crap by himself. Ask him if he considers himself lucky. Trust me. He'll say yes. Every time. He has persuaded himself he's the luckiest guy in the world. But he's not. You know why?

*Pause.*

Because I am.

DR. GUZMAN     Everything happens sequentially. Music. DNA. Every story ever told. There is an order to the universe. If chicken, then egg. Or if egg, then chicken. And, even more importantly, the order implies causality. Egg creates chicken. Or chicken spawns egg.

THEO     What determines success? Does a Nobel Prize recipient stand up and say, "I'm an average schmuck who just got lucky"? No, they won't tell you that. But I will. Because in many ways I'm just like you. I put on my pants one leg at a time—always the right one first, as someone once pointed out to me.

DR. GUZMAN     But whatever you do, do not tell me it doesn't matter. That's a cheat. The only thing I detest more than cheating is laziness, and chaos is lazy. Entropy is lazy. God is lazy.

*DR. GUZMAN circles the word GOD.*

THEO     Except, on the luck scale, I am off the charts. If you look at the odds I've fortuitously overcome... I'm told I'm a one in a billion. That's with a B!

DR. GUZMAN

Order is sweat. Order is who you are and why you're here today. In this classroom. On this planet. Wasting oxygen.

*THEO holds up a book.*

THEO

My book is called *Change Your Luck*. And *that* is the reason you're here today.

DR. GUZMAN

So which came first? You may not know right now, but by the end of my class you *will* hypothesize an answer, support it, and commit to it.

*She underlines WHICH CAME FIRST.*

THEO

There are a thousand books out there that offer to change you in some way. Change your attitude. Your diet. Your golf swing. You know the best way to shave a couple of strokes off your score?

*Pause.*

Get a hole in one.

*THEO circles the word LUCK.*

DR. GUZMAN

I'm telling you right now, you'd better start thinking about it. The last question on your final exam will be this... Which came first? A: the chicken. B: the egg. C: simultaneous. And if anyone is audacious or careless enough to put down C, that will earn you an automatic F and you will be shot. I know you've heard those campus myths about me. Don't test me. I have tenure.

THEO         Now before we get started, let me ask you a question.

> *DR. GUZMAN reaches for a white cane, smacks it against her hand.*

DR. GUZMAN      What jury would convict a blind woman?

> *THEO reaches into a jar full of papers.*

THEO         Anybody feel lucky today?

> *The board shows:*

> *WHICH CAME FIRST?*

> *LUCK         GOD*

## Laboratory

> *DR. GUZMAN holds a clipboard close to her eyes.*

> *She has good central vision but no peripheral vision. She has learned to compensate.*

> *A knock on the door.*

DR. GUZMAN      Who is it?

MR. ADAMSON   *(off stage)* Dr. Guzman? I'm one of your students. From your 121 class.

DR. GUZMAN      What time is it?

MR. ADAMSON    *(off stage)* I'm sorry, I know it's late. But the library just closed and I thought I'd take a chance. You don't have regular office hours.

DR. GUZMAN    See me after class.

MR. ADAMSON    *(off stage)* By the time I get to the front you're out the door.

DR. GUZMAN    Walk faster.

MR. ADAMSON    *(off stage)* Right.

      *Pause.*

You said you wanted to see me.

DR. GUZMAN    Give me your ID card.

      *She slips the clipboard under the door.*

      *When she pulls back the clipboard there is an ID card on it. She holds it close to her eyes, then stuffs it in her pocket.*

Ah, Mr. Adamson. I've been looking forward to meeting you.

      *DR. GUZMAN unlocks the door and opens it. She slips the key back into her pocket.*

You'd think with the recent incidents the university could spring for some state-of-the-art security. I'd settle for a damn peephole.

*MR. ADAMSON enters.*

*He is in a wheelchair, a jacket on his lap.*

A wheelchair. Intriguing.

*MR. ADAMSON reaches for his jacket.*

*Without warning, DR. GUZMAN grabs the jacket, tosses it aside, and reveals a briefcase.*

*She lunges for the briefcase, throws it on her desk.*

Put your hands on your head. I said put your hands on your head.

*MR. ADAMSON reluctantly lifts his arms.*

*DR. GUZMAN does her best to frisk him. She kneels down, looks under the wheelchair.*

Hear the latest? Some undergrad student sneaks into a genetics laboratory at Princeton and burns the whole thing down. Shoots the Ph.D., who just happened to be a stem-cell researcher. We seem to be a dying breed.

*DR. GUZMAN turns her attention to the briefcase. It's locked.*

What's the combination?

MR. ADAMSON    I'd prefer if you didn't open it.

DR. GUZMAN   I'd prefer if I was assigned to teach courses commensurate with my qualifications. What's the combination? No doubt something you might be capable of memorizing... One two three, four five six? What's inside?

> *No response.* DR. GUZMAN *tries various combinations on the briefcase lock.*

MR. ADAMSON   Can I please have my briefcase?

DR. GUZMAN   I have reviewed the results of the Introductory Genetics final exam.

MR. ADAMSON   It was a long test.

DR. GUZMAN   I like to separate the men from the boys.

MR. ADAMSON   So which am I?

DR. GUZMAN   You, Mr. Adamson, are an embryo. No, a zygote. That first moment when the sperm touches a polysaccharide on the egg and says, "Hi honey, I'm home." That instant when the staunchest pro-lifer in all of Kentucky would have a tough time calling it the beginning of human life. That's what you are.

MR. ADAMSON   So did I pass?

> DR. GUZMAN *draws a bell curve on the board. She doesn't let go of the briefcase.*

DR. GUZMAN   In this exam, the mean was seventy-one per cent. The passing grade was fifty-eight. Sixteen per cent got an A.

*She draws on the board: 16.*

MR. ADAMSON   What did I get?

DR. GUZMAN   You got an F.

MR. ADAMSON   I see.

DR. GUZMAN   Sometimes you get an outlier on the curve. On this exam, one person ended up more than five standard deviations below the mean. Do you know what that means?

MR. ADAMSON   No.

DR. GUZMAN   Computer malfunction. Usually. Only this time, the computer was right. You, sir, had the misfortune of getting *every question wrong*.

## Auditorium

*THEO packs up his briefcase on stage.*

*CYNTHIA enters. She is not used to wearing a mini-skirt and she is not flirtatious.*

CYNTHIA   I don't believe in luck.

THEO You must be Cynthia.

CYNTHIA They sure cleared out the auditorium in a hurry.

THEO Kickoff is in an hour and a half. I'm surprised anyone even came. I'm Theo.

CYNTHIA I know who you are. I just sat through your speech, or whatever you call that.

THEO You look familiar. Have we met before?

CYNTHIA Are you hitting on me?

THEO Excuse me?

CYNTHIA I don't believe in luck.

THEO I don't believe in unicorns with paisley headbands.

CYNTHIA I'm serious.

THEO So what brings you here then?

CYNTHIA I'm here because you selected me.

THEO Randomly.

CYNTHIA It would seem.

THEO If I had pulled another name out of the jar, I could be having an equally engaging conversation with a little old lady from Tallahassee.

CYNTHIA     But you wouldn't want to sleep with her.

THEO        No. *Probably* not.

CYNTHIA     Isn't that what this is about?

THEO        You won a book. In a draw. That's what this is about.
            You got lucky, that's all.

            *THEO pulls out a book and a pen.*

            Who should I make this out to?

CYNTHIA     There must have been a thousand people in this place.
            Assuming half of them actually wanted to meet you,
            that means there were five hundred names in that jar.

THEO        Why assume half?

CYNTHIA     I just assumed the other half might have to get back
            to the nursing home. Have a sponge bath.

THEO        I'll bet you there were a thousand names in that
            jar. But I know it's not about me. Or my book. It's
            about the winning. Everybody wants to be lucky. Or
            luckier. As I say in the book, luck is like your penis.
            You can always use a little more. Except for me, of
            course.

CYNTHIA     Of course. You're the luckiest man alive.

THEO        Exactly. But that's why people showed up today. I
            have something everybody wants. They want my

luck. They believe it's contagious. Or somehow transmissible.

CYNTHIA        By exchange of bodily fluids?

THEO           Some do. And if some young woman in need of a little luck feels some of mine might rub off on her...

CYNTHIA        By rubbing off on you.

THEO           Then who am I to argue?

CYNTHIA        A self-serving father figure who thinks he's God's gift?

*THEO scribbles something in the book.*

THEO           Don't be so quick to judge. One day *you* might find yourself in a position where you need a little luck.

*THEO hands the book to CYNTHIA, puts on his jacket.*

CYNTHIA        But I wouldn't be so naive as to think fooling around with some self-professed lucky guy would win me the lottery.

*She reads the inscription.*

"To Cynthia. Good luck. From God's gift."

THEO           Theodore does mean "gift of God."

*CYNTHIA tosses the book to the floor.*

CYNTHIA     I think we both know I'm not here by luck alone.

THEO        Then why *are* you here? Just a coincidence?

## Laboratory

MR. ADAMSON   No way. Every question?

> *DR. GUZMAN continues to try combinations on the briefcase.*

> *MR. ADAMSON looks for an opportunity to take it back.*

DR. GUZMAN    Even the last one.

MR. ADAMSON   I got zero per cent?

DR. GUZMAN    Ha! If only. An exam should assess one's knowledge, not one's luck. Did you guess, Mr. Adamson?

MR. ADAMSON   It depends on what you mean by guessing.

DR. GUZMAN    I mean, did you throw a dart or two? Or a hundred and fifty?

MR. ADAMSON   I did my best.

DR. GUZMAN    If you had bothered to read the instructions, you would have realized that, to deter guessing, this examination was scored in a right-minus-wrong fashion.

MR. ADAMSON      Uh oh.

DR. GUZMAN       Your mark, Mr. Adamson, was *negative* one fifty.

                 *She draws an emphatic negative line on the board.*

MR. ADAMSON      I thought you graded on a curve.

DR. GUZMAN       Mr. Adamson, for any kind of curve to help you, it
                 would have to have been the statistical equivalent of
                 Marilyn Monroe being sucked into a black hole. You
                 even got the last question wrong. I thought I made it
                 clear. C, simultaneous, is not the answer. It's almost
                 as if you were trying to fail this exam.

MR. ADAMSON      Why would I try to fail?

DR. GUZMAN       Why indeed. After I saw your result, as an exper-
                 iment, I asked my graduate class to take this
                 examination. And I assigned them the task of
                 getting the *lowest* mark they could. The brightest
                 guy in my group actually got *four* questions *right*.
                 By accident! So how does some generic undergrad
                 student earn the worst achievable score in my final
                 examination?

MR. ADAMSON      What do you mean, "generic"?

DR. GUZMAN       Hmmm. Good question.

                 *DR. GUZMAN pulls a voice recorder from her pocket.*

*(into voice recorder)* Can one be both generic and handicapped, or are the two mutually exclusive? Fascinating...

MR. ADAMSON    Dr. Guzman, I'm a little confused. You wanted to see me because I got every question wrong? Is that why?

DR. GUZMAN    I wanted to meet you, Mr. Adamson, because there are only four possible answers. A, you're exceptionally smart. B, you're exceptionally stupid. C, you're exceptionally unlucky. Or D, and I sincerely hope this is not the case, you cheated. Can you conceive of any other alternatives?

## Auditorium

CYNTHIA    A coincidence? That word is incense laced with crack. Or vice versa.

*THEO picks up his briefcase.*

THEO    You don't believe in coincidences?

CYNTHIA    Sure I believe in them. They happen every day. Simply a random statistical event that occurs no more or less frequently than the models predict. It's called a co-incidence. Not a cause-incidence.

THEO    Guess what? My dog's name is Cynthia.

*THEO tries to leave. CYNTHIA blocks his path. Repeatedly.*

CYNTHIA     So what? There are twenty thousand Cynthias roaming this country. The chances are pretty good you'll cross paths with one of us sooner or later. I am so sick of people seeing a predictable co-incidence as some sort of wormhole into the mystical side of the universe. It's not very sexy and it clashes with everyone's yoga pants, but the truth is, your dog and I just happen to be in the same subset and our paths intersected today.

THEO        But just because there's a chance of something happening, that doesn't mean it's going to happen. You still need a little luck.

CYNTHIA     No, all you need is a little *math*. Talk to Pascal.

THEO        Who's Pascal?

CYNTHIA     Grandfather of probability theory. Have you heard of Pascal's Triangle? Pascal's Wager?

THEO        Rings a bell.

CYNTHIA     Pascal would tell you, while the odds of you bumping into a Cynthia right here and now are miniscule, the odds of something *like that* happening are high. Even *probable*. Guess what? I have a goldfish named Theodore. Woooo. The universe must be trying to tell us something. Maybe we should compare zodiac signs. I'm a Scorpio, what are you? No, wait... I might be an Aquarius. You know what impresses me more than coincidence?

THEO        Name-dropping historical figures?

CYNTHIA     A lack of coincidence. Assuming one possible event
            per second, each of us can expect a one-in-a-million
            miracle every month. Now, if you manage to make
            it through this whole month *without* bumping into a
            Cynthia, *then* call up the papers and tell them about
            the coincidence that *never happened.*

THEO        Math major?

            *THEO finally reaches the door.*

CYNTHIA     Biology major, math minor, I mean, haven't you
            ever noticed you can only identify a coincidence in
            hindsight? But the best way to prove any scientific
            theory is to *predict* the outcome. If you'd woken up
            this morning and declared, "Today at 3:20 p.m., I'm
            going to meet a left-handed woman with a gold-
            fish named Theo, who will inexplicably grab my
            briefcase…"

            *CYNTHIA grabs THEO's briefcase, runs away.*

            Now I'm interested!

THEO        Do you really have a goldfish named Theo?

CYNTHIA     You're not getting this, are you?

THEO        I knew someone who died on her birthday. You have
            to admit, that seems coincidental. Can I have my
            briefcase back?

CYNTHIA     Do you know what the odds are of dying on your
            birthday?

THEO           Let me see. One in 365?

CYNTHIA        Actually, one in 321.

THEO           Really? Why's that?

CYNTHIA        I don't know. My point is, dying on your birthday is
               no big deal. Statistically speaking. Shakespeare died
               on his birthday. Three people in the audience today
               will die on their birthday.

THEO           Maybe you.

CYNTHIA        Maybe me. But that doesn't mean the universe is
               trying to tell us something.

THEO           Fine, but you're here. In this room. Holding my brief-
               case. Why? Why here? Why now? It can't just be
               random chance, can it?

CYNTHIA        It can. But it isn't. There's another possibility.

## Laboratory

DR. GUZMAN     Let's examine the options. A. You're exceptionally
               smart. I think we can safely exclude that possibility.

               *DR. GUZMAN searches for a screwdriver.*

MR. ADAMSON    Based on what? My wheelchair?

DR. GUZMAN  Right, Professor Hawking, it's about your wheelchair. I'm just saying that if you are smart enough to get all the questions wrong, then I would expect you'd be smart enough to get them all right. I have no idea why an aspiring scientist would aim for negative one fifty.

MR. ADAMSON  So now you're calling me stupid?

DR. GUZMAN  Actually, no. If you were stupid enough to guess on all one hundred and fifty questions, you should still have gotten thirty-seven right. So, I ask myself, did you cheat? But for the life of me, I can't figure out why anyone would cheat to get the worst possible score. Can you?

MR. ADAMSON  No.

DR. GUZMAN  If you cheat on my exam, that tells me you think you're smarter than me. Do you think you're smarter than me, Mr. Adamson?

MR. ADAMSON  No.

DR. GUZMAN  So you're just unlucky. Exceptionally unlucky.

MR. ADAMSON  I don't believe in luck.

DR. GUZMAN  And I don't believe in handing over cheaters to that pansy-assed dean for a slap on the wrist.

MR. ADAMSON  I didn't cheat.

DR. GUZMAN    Well, it has to be one or the other, and I intend to find out which.

## Auditorium

CYNTHIA    What if… I'm here today because I wanted to be here?

> THEO *tries to get his briefcase back, but* CYNTHIA *stays one step ahead.*

> *Although* CYNTHIA *moves throughout the room, she conspicuously avoids walking under the ladder.*

THEO    There are 999 other people who wanted to be here.

CYNTHIA    Give or take. But maybe these 999 rocket scientists were so busy reading chapter seven, "Change Your Luck by Changing the Way You Wipe Your Ass," that they neglected to exercise their free will.

THEO    So you willed your way into being selected? Maybe I should read *your* book. How exactly does one overcome the one-in-a-thousand odds?

CYNTHIA    Let's see. Perhaps one could surreptitiously replace all the slips of paper in the jar with a bunch of new ones. I mean, really, is anyone going to pull out a second name to confirm the validity of the draw?

THEO    Are you saying you cheated?

CYNTHIA    Or maybe one could use one's analytical mind to consider that in both of your other readings this week, the "random draw" just happened to select a young woman in the front row who was wearing a miniskirt.

THEO    Are you saying *I* cheated?

CYNTHIA    Did you?

THEO    Maybe I just got lucky.

CYNTHIA    The chances of you selecting three young women wearing miniskirts from the front row, by chance alone, even assuming an *optimistic* ten per cent miniskirt coefficient is one in two billion.

THEO    It's not zero.

CYNTHIA    It's never zero. Unless it's impossible.

THEO    So you're saying I'm lucky.

CYNTHIA    Unbelievably lucky.

THEO    That's what I've been telling you!

    *Pause.*

    Did you actually sit through my talk three times?

CYNTHIA    Yes.

THEO    Why? Are you a stalker?

> *THEO corners CYNTHIA behind the ladder. Her only apparent option is to duck under the ladder. She hesitates.*

CYNTHIA      Define stalker.

THEO      Why three times?

CYNTHIA      I was trying to decide.

> *Abruptly, CYNTHIA scrambles up the ladder, still holding the briefcase.*

THEO      Decide what?

> *CYNTHIA sits on top of the ladder, briefcase on her lap.*

CYNTHIA      Whether to wear a miniskirt.

THEO      Excellent decision.

CYNTHIA      Evidently. But I'm not going to sleep with you.

THEO      Zero chance?

CYNTHIA      Let's call it one in ten to the forty-ninth.

THEO      That's not zero. Right?

CYNTHIA      All you have to do is persuade me that sleeping with you will give me everything my little heart desires. Then yes, it's a non-zero probability.

> *THEO reaches into his inside jacket pocket. He produces a small bottle.*

THEO      Champagne?

CYNTHIA      I shouldn't. I'm pregnant.

## Laboratory

DR. GUZMAN      What are the odds? Mr. Adamson, do you know what the chances are of getting all one hundred and fifty questions wrong, purely by guessing? About the same chance as throwing sixty-three coins on the ground and having them *all* come up heads. *One in five quintillion.*

> *DR. GUZMAN finds a screwdriver, tries using it to open the briefcase.*

So you see? I don't mean to insult you by calling you unlucky. It's a fact, not an opinion.

MR. ADAMSON      I disagree.

DR. GUZMAN      There is no other explanation.

MR. ADAMSON      There is.

DR. GUZMAN      Educate me.

MR. ADAMSON      Maybe it was God's will.

DR. GUZMAN    God?

*She backs away from him, finds her white cane.*

My unannounced late-night caller is a religious nut?
This gets better and better.

MR. ADAMSON    I'm not a nut.

DR. GUZMAN    If I didn't know better, I'd think you were here under
false pretenses.

MR. ADAMSON    I'm here because you said you wanted to see me. If
we're all finished here—

DR. GUZMAN    Mr. Adamson, would you consider yourself unlucky?

MR. ADAMSON    Absolutely not.

DR. GUZMAN    Have you ever won anything?

MR. ADAMSON    I won the heart of a girl once. But she left me for
someone who could walk. Darn walkers.

DR. GUZMAN    Anything random? A raffle? A toaster? Two tickets
to a monster-truck show?

MR. ADAMSON    No, can't say I have.

DR. GUZMAN    Ever play a slot machine? Roulette? The lottery?

MR. ADAMSON    I've bought a lottery ticket every week for the last
seven years.

DR. GUZMAN     What have you won?

MR. ADAMSON   I won a free ticket once. That was pretty exciting. I thought it was a sign.

DR. GUZMAN     Was it?

MR. ADAMSON   No.

*MR. ADAMSON checks the watch on his right hand.*

What time is it? I really should get going, it's getting kinda—

DR. GUZMAN     Why are you in a wheelchair?

MR. ADAMSON   Because I can't walk.

DR. GUZMAN     Thank you, Captain Pike, that's very helpful.

MR. ADAMSON   I was born with cerebral palsy. Doctors said I would never walk. But I proved them wrong. By my twelfth birthday I was actually the fastest kid on my football team.

DR. GUZMAN     Congratulations.

MR. ADAMSON   By thirteen I was back in a wheelchair.

DR. GUZMAN     What happened?

MR. ADAMSON   Drunk driver ran a crosswalk.

DR. GUZMAN     No shit.

MR. ADAMSON     There were eight of us crossing. Everybody else walked away. Doctors said I would never walk again. I didn't believe them.

DR. GUZMAN     *(into voice recorder)* Cerebral palsy, one in three hundred. Drunk driver, one in eight.

MR. ADAMSON     You think I'm unlucky?

DR. GUZMAN     You think you're not?

MR. ADAMSON     I think God makes everything happen for a reason. If I wasn't disabled I probably wouldn't even be here talking to you. I'm pretty sure I only got admission because I'd look good in class pictures.

## Auditorium

THEO     And that's why you're here today. Because you're pregnant.

CYNTHIA     That's a little presumptuous.

THEO     Something made you put on that miniskirt. I'll bet it has something to do with your baby. Am I right?

    *CYNTHIA doesn't respond.*

    First child?

CYNTHIA     First pregnancy. And last. I am not going through this again.

THEO   Morning sickness?

CYNTHIA  I can deal with the morning sickness. I just... I swore I wouldn't put myself in this situation.

THEO   What situation?

CYNTHIA  You wouldn't understand.

THEO   Yeah, you're probably right.

CYNTHIA  The situation where I'm sitting on a ladder wearing a miniskirt, talking to some guy who claims he's the luckiest man in the world... all because of this.

    *CYNTHIA produces an envelope.*

THEO   What's that?

    *CYNTHIA doesn't answer.*

    I'll bet you want my help with that.

CYNTHIA  You like to bet, don't you?

THEO   That's what we do, we lucky people.

CYNTHIA  According to *60 Minutes*, you made your first bet twenty years ago.

    *CYNTHIA puts away the envelope.*

THEO   Yes, I believe that was Super Bowl xyz-lmnop.

CYNTHIA        Don't most people bet on who's going to win?

THEO           My way, you didn't have to worry about silly things
               like who had the better team.

CYNTHIA        So that's why you bet on the coin flip.

THEO           That was the only place on the planet I could actually
               make a bet like that. A true fifty-fifty proposition.

CYNTHIA        Flipping a coin is not a true fifty-fifty proposition.

THEO           I've been misled.

               *CYNTHIA climbs down from the ladder, still protect-*
               *ing the briefcase. She makes her way to the board.*

CYNTHIA        For starters, there is a one in six thousand chance
               of a coin landing on its edge, so it's more like 49.99
               each way. But that aside, if you start with a coin
               showing tails up, there is a greater likelihood of it
               ending tails up.

THEO           How do you figure that?

               *CYNTHIA draws on the board a coin, rotating in air.*

CYNTHIA        The coin rotates in the air… Tails, then heads, then
               tails… Overall, it spends fractionally more time in
               tails than in heads.

THEO           I should have bet tails.

CYNTHIA        You did. Twenty years ago. A thousand dollars. Every penny you had to your name.

THEO          I felt lucky.

CYNTHIA        Doubled your money.

THEO          I *was* lucky.

CYNTHIA        Same thing the following year. Only heads. Why heads?

THEO          Why not?

CYNTHIA        Doubled your money. Again. Now four grand. Next year, tails. Then tails. Then heads. Double or nothing every time. Don't believe in hedging your bets?

THEO          I was on a roll.

CYNTHIA        You're not kidding. Every Super Bowl since you've bet on the coin toss. And every year, for the last twenty years, you have doubled your money.

THEO          More or less. Casinos take a cut. Bookies take a cut.

CYNTHIA        Last January you placed a bet of 440 *million* dollars on heads. And won.

## Laboratory

DR. GUZMAN    That's ridiculous. Your God's bright idea is that he bestows upon you paraplegia as your ticket to the Ivy League?

MR. ADAMSON    Isn't that why you're here?

DR. GUZMAN    What are you implying?

MR. ADAMSON    I figured if anybody would understand it would be you. Can I please have my briefcase back?

DR. GUZMAN    Are you suggesting I'm here because I've lost ninety-two per cent of my peripheral vision?

MR. ADAMSON    No, of course not. Your success is clearly due to your achievements. But in the beginning...

DR. GUZMAN    In the beginning? Isn't that the opening line of Darwin's *On the Origin of Species*? No, that's not it.

MR. ADAMSON    I was just wondering if your disability might have helped you. When you were starting out. A foot in the door.

DR. GUZMAN    Because my white cane might look good in class pictures.

MR. ADAMSON    I'm sorry. I didn't mean—

| DR. GUZMAN | You have the audacity to suggest my blindness is somehow an advantageous mutation? Do you have any idea what I've had to overcome to be here? The sacrifices I've made for *this*? |

> *DR. GUZMAN gestures to her lab.*

|  | If *you* knew you were going to be completely blind within a year, what would you be staring at right now? Tropical sunsets? Impressionist paintings? Or test tubes? |

| MR. ADAMSON | Why don't you just stop? Go see the world, before… |

| DR. GUZMAN | Before I can't see the world? Because if I stop now, Mr. Adamson, I will have wasted my sight on a failed experiment and that would mean I earned an F. But, unlike you, I have no intention of spending my remaining days lying awake at night second-guessing my choices. |

| MR. ADAMSON | I don't do that. |

| DR. GUZMAN | You never think about that chance rendezvous with the car? I don't believe that. |

| MR. ADAMSON | I try not to. But you know what I do think about? All those little things I could have done that day that might have slowed me down half a step. If I had to tie my shoelace. Or even just sneeze. But what's there to second-guess? How could I have known? |

DR. GUZMAN     I knew. I saw the darkness creeping in from the corners. And I chose to lock myself in this basement lab. I chose science. Over sunsets.

MR. ADAMSON     Some people might second-guess that.

DR. GUZMAN     I am not some people. I knew I had the brains and the ambition and opportunity to attempt something significant. Better a bold F than a timid W. Only now, they're calling me unstable! An intellectual liability. They're looking for an excuse to put me out to pasture, while I work day and night to make my mark, before I lose the remaining eight per cent of my visual field.

MR. ADAMSON     Dr. Guzman, there's a pub down the street. With a ramp. How about I buy you a drink?

DR. GUZMAN     Mr. Adamson, do you want to walk again?

MR. ADAMSON     I don't need to walk again to have a meaningful life.

DR. GUZMAN     Answer the question.

MR. ADAMSON     I will walk again when God decides—

DR. GUZMAN     A. You want to walk again. B. You don't.

MR. ADAMSON     A.

DR. GUZMAN     I may be able to help you.

MR. ADAMSON     I'm not interested in spinal-cord research.

MR. ADAMSON     Genetics. I don't believe in genetics.

          *MR. ADAMSON moves around the room, incon-*
          *spicuously holding up his cellphone, searching for*
          *reception.*

DR. GUZMAN     That's preposterous. Our genes are the very building blocks of life. The order of the four base pairs in your DNA has programmed everything about you. That sequence created you.

MR. ADAMSON     I don't know. It seems kind of arbitrary.

DR. GUZMAN     Arbitrary? Without order there is chaos.

MR. ADAMSON     Without God there is chaos. The DNA is just... calligraphy.

DR. GUZMAN     There is order to DNA. Just like there is order to everything. What if Beethoven played every note in his fifth symphony simultaneously? How would that sound? Without order it's not a symphony, it's a cacophony.

MR. ADAMSON     Maybe it's just a different piece of music.

DR. GUZMAN     No, I'm pretty sure it's a cacophony.

MR. ADAMSON     Order is subjective. It doesn't matter what order the ten commandments are written in.

DR. GUZMAN     Really? They're not prioritized? How sloppy! I would have used a logarithmic scale to compensate for the relative value discrepancy of killing versus merely coveting.

MR. ADAMSON     Wouldn't change their meaning. The sequence was not part of the design.

DR. GUZMAN     But a gene, like any text, is not a palindrome. If you read *Hamlet* backwards, what do you have?

MR. ADAMSON     Tel... mah?

DR. GUZMAN     You'd have gibberish. There is order in everything. Just ask Watson and Crick.

MR. ADAMSON     Why not Crick and Watson? The order is meaningless. It's the chicken and the egg.

*DR. GUZMAN draws a B on the board.*

DR. GUZMAN     Actually, it's the egg and chicken. The correct answer was B.

The egg came first.

*Pause.*

Mr. Adamson, how much more research will you require to establish, with a p-value of less than 0.05, that there is no cellphone signal down here?

MR. ADAMSON     Dr. Guzman, what did you mean when you said you might be able to help me?

DR. GUZMAN     How badly do you want to walk?

MR. ADAMSON     What do you mean, on a scale of one to ten?

DR. GUZMAN      If I gave you two new legs right now, what's the first thing you'd do?

MR. ADAMSON     I'd probably take the door key from your pocket.

DR. GUZMAN      You don't want my help.

MR. ADAMSON     I guess I'd try to meet a girl.

DR. GUZMAN      Right. You've never had sex.

MR. ADAMSON     It's not about sex.

DR. GUZMAN      Everything's about sex. Ask Darwin.

MR. ADAMSON     Sure, I want to experience… that. After I get married, of course. And fall in love.

DR. GUZMAN      Of course.

MR. ADAMSON     I want to be a dad.

DR. GUZMAN      You don't need new legs for that. If your reproductive organs are still intact they can extract the sperm.

MR. ADAMSON     Sounds romantic.

DR. GUZMAN      There could be scented candles. Vivaldi. Perhaps a moonlight extraction.

MR. ADAMSON     If God wants me to have kids, He will make it happen naturally.

DR. GUZMAN   So if He decides you're worthy of having children, He will first make you walk.

MR. ADAMSON   Yes.

DR. GUZMAN   You know your God is rolling his eyes right now.

MR. ADAMSON   I don't think you can help me.

> *DR. GUZMAN reaches into a beaker full of coins. She produces a single coin.*

DR. GUZMAN   Tell you what, Mr. One-in-Five-Quintillion. Call it. Heads or tails. If you get it right, you can go.

## Auditorium

CYNTHIA   Really?

THEO   Call it a hunch.

CYNTHIA   You have a hunch you're going to guess wrong? Today?

THEO   Yes.

CYNTHIA   Do you think that every year?

THEO   First time.

CYNTHIA   So don't place your bet. Just leave your money in the bank. Why risk it?

THEO    He who lives by the coin flip should die by the coin flip. Don't you think?

CYNTHIA    No! That makes no sense. If you think you're going to lose, quit while you're ahead. Thank your lucky stars and ride off into the sunset. That's the smart thing to do.

THEO    I never said I was the *smartest* guy alive.

CYNTHIA    Don't be ridiculous. What if you lose? Have you even thought about that?

THEO    Every day.

CYNTHIA    You'd become some ordinary guy whose luck and greed eventually caught up with him. No fame. No fortune. You'd lose everything.

THEO    Just an ordinary guy.

CYNTHIA    But if you don't place the bet, you'd walk away a winner. You'd still be the luckiest man alive.

THEO    Until I die.

CYNTHIA    Isn't that what you want?

THEO    I'll let you in on a little secret. This time tomorrow, I'll be a billionaire. Or I'll be broke. But either way, win or lose, it's going to end. Today's going to be my last bet.

CYNTHIA    I thought they wouldn't let you stop.

THEO             If I lose, they won't care. If I win… well, this time
                 I won't give them a choice.

CYNTHIA          Then why not stop now? Why roll the dice one last
                 time? You could lose it all today.

THEO             I know.

CYNTHIA          Well, Mr. Super-Lucky-Man, if it makes you feel
                 any better, I don't think you're going to lose today.

                 *CYNTHIA hands THEO his briefcase.*

                 I've figured out your secret.

## Laboratory

MR. ADAMSON      So tell me. What's the catch?

DR. GUZMAN       The catch is, if you guess *wrong* on the coin flip, there
                 will be a consequence.

MR. ADAMSON      Excuse me?

DR. GUZMAN       Without stakes, how can we truly evaluate the
                 "unlucky" hypothesis?

MR. ADAMSON      So this is some kind of test?

DR. GUZMAN       An experiment, if you will. A critical assessment of
                 your luck. Or lack thereof.

MR. ADAMSON    What do you mean, consequence?

DR. GUZMAN    I'm sure we can think of something. I know I have a bottle of H2SO4 here somewhere.

MR. ADAMSON    H2SO4?

DR. GUZMAN    Sulphuric acid. So which is it? Heads or tails?

MR. ADAMSON    Why the egg? Why did the egg come first?

DR. GUZMAN    Ah. We know all new species appear via mutation. Since DNA can only be modified prenatally, the first chicken egg gave birth to the first chicken.

> MR. ADAMSON *comes across a phone jack in the wall. He follows the wire.*

MR. ADAMSON    But a chicken laid the egg in the first place.

DR. GUZMAN    No. A creature which was similar to a chicken, but technically not a chicken, laid that first egg. Likely the Red Junglefowl.

> DR. GUZMAN *finds a stethoscope, uses it to listen to the briefcase lock.*

MR. ADAMSON    Fine, but which came first, the Red Junglefowl or the egg?

DR. GUZMAN    The egg. Same logic. Wouldn't you agree?

MR. ADAMSON    No. I would not. "And God said, Let the waters bring forth abundantly the moving creature that hath life, and fowl that may fly above the earth in the open firmament of Heaven."

DR. GUZMAN      So your money is on the chicken.

MR. ADAMSON     My money is on God. It doesn't matter whether God created the egg first or the chicken first. It's irrelevant. It doesn't matter if it's Watson and Crick. Baskin and Robbins. Ernie and Bert.

DR. GUZMAN      Bert and Ernie. Only thirteen per cent of the population says Ernie and Bert.

> *As DR. GUZMAN writes 13% on the board, MR. ADAMSON follows the phone wire to a desk.*

MR. ADAMSON     Did you get a research grant to study that?

DR. GUZMAN      Somebody did. What I'm saying is, everything has an order. It's fundamental. It's intrinsic. The order is everything.

> *Under some papers on the desk, MR. ADAMSON finds a cordless phone base.*

MR. ADAMSON     Why does it matter if it's Ernie and Bert or Bert and Ernie? They're still the same people.

DR. GUZMAN      Muppets. Ernie has no DNA. Ernie has no parents. Ernie has no God.

MR. ADAMSON     Everything has a God.

DR. GUZMAN      Even Oscar the Grouch?

MR. ADAMSON    Even you.

*The cordless phone locator alarm beeps.*

*DR. GUZMAN holds up the phone handset.*

DR. GUZMAN    Looking for this?

*She climbs the ladder, places the phone on a shelf, out of his reach.*

We have a hypothesis to test. Heads or tails, Mr. Adamson.

MR. ADAMSON    Why not tails or heads?

DR. GUZMAN    Ha! So what you're saying is, it doesn't matter. We all put our pants on one leg at a time. Whether it's your right leg first or your left, the order doesn't matter, right?

MR. ADAMSON    You still end up wearing pants.

DR. GUZMAN    Ah, but that's where you're wrong. It does matter. Would you believe which pant leg you put on first is a question that has significant scientific implications? And, it's predictable.

MR. ADAMSON    Are you telling me you can predict which leg I put on first?

## Auditorium

THEO    What's the secret?

*CYNTHIA draws on the board: Hs and Ts.*

CYNTHIA    I've been analyzing your picks. Tails. Heads. Tails. Tails. Heads. Heads. Heads. Tails tails tails tails tails heads heads heads heads heads heads heads, and, last year, heads.

THEO    I'm honoured. And disturbed.

*THEO nudges toward the door.*

CYNTHIA    Notice anything interesting?

THEO    About what?

CYNTHIA    About the sequence.

THEO    Like what?

CYNTHIA    How do you make your picks?

THEO    I pick them out of a hat.

CYNTHIA    Bullshit!

THEO    If you really must know, I make my picks by flipping a coin.

CYNTHIA   You pick the result of the coin flip by actually flipping a coin?

THEO   Seemed appropriate.

CYNTHIA   So you take your lucky coin...

THEO   No, I lost my "lucky coin" after year six. So now I use any old coin. It's not the coin that's lucky. Although, I will say, year seven was a bit suspenseful.

CYNTHIA   And you flip it.

THEO   Once a year.

CYNTHIA   And by flipping that coin you got that sequence. Tails. Heads. Tails. Tails. Et cetera.

THEO   The last eight have been heads.

CYNTHIA   Yes. That's quite a feat in itself. Do you know what the odds are of getting eight heads in a row? One in 256.

THEO   Most people are betting on nine in a row. The odds in Vegas are six to five for heads this year.

CYNTHIA   Are you telling me millions of people collectively believe that because you've had eight heads in a row you're more likely to have nine?

THEO   Hundreds of millions.

CYNTHIA   Idiots!

THEO            Why are they idiots? How do you know they're
                wrong?

CYNTHIA         They're being seduced by the last eight heads. But
                the odds of the next one being heads remains one
                in two.

THEO            They still might be right.

> THEO *checks his watch. He wears it on his right wrist.*

What time is it? I should make my pick.

CYNTHIA         This year, I'd pick tails.

THEO            Why tails?

CYNTHIA         Trust me.

THEO            If you're so convinced, why don't you put your money
                where your mouth is?

> THEO *opens the door.*

CYNTHIA         Okay. If it comes up heads, I'll sleep with you.

> THEO *stops.*

THEO            Go on.

CYNTHIA         Let's examine your sequence mathematically. One
                tails. One heads. Two tails. Three heads. Five tails.
                Eight heads. One one two three five eight.

*She circles groups of Hs and Ts, then writes 1 1 2 3 5 8.*

THEO     That's my briefcase combination. One one two, three five eight.

CYNTHIA     Are you serious? Why that number?

THEO     I've always used that number, ever since I was a kid.

*THEO looks at his watch.*

CYNTHIA     Do you know what that is? One one two three five eight. It's the first six numbers of the Fibonacci sequence... the most fundamental and universal mathematical sequence ever identified!

## Laboratory

DR. GUZMAN     Your right. Then your left.

*MR. ADAMSON tries on an imaginary set of pants.*

MR. ADAMSON     How do you know that?

*MR. ADAMSON circles the room, looking for something he can use to reach the phone.*

DR. GUZMAN     Over the course of our lifetime, we will put on our pants forty thousand times. And whether it's right then left, or vice versa, do you know how many times the average person will do it in reverse? Never! From the age of six, we are absolutely faithful to that order. Try doing it backwards sometime. See how awkward it feels. How alien. But why? How does a child even learn which leg to put on first?

MR. ADAMSON   From their mom?

DR. GUZMAN   Precisely! But not how you think. For fraternal twins, the concordance rate on the pant leg order was sixty per cent. In identical twins... ninety-eight per cent. *Ergo...*

MR. ADAMSON   Are you trying to tell me if I put my pants on right leg first, that's genetic? That's crazy.

DR. GUZMAN   I've identified the PLO gene.

MR. ADAMSON   PLO?

DR. GUZMAN   Pant Leg Order. It's X-linked. You get it from your mom, who got it from her dad. I'm hoping to publish the results. If I can make it past the damn peer review.

MR. ADAMSON   I'm sure the Nobel Prize committee will be all over this.

*MR. ADAMSON finds a book on the floor.*

DR. GUZMAN   How dare you. I've spent a significant portion of my professional career unearthing this gene.

MR. ADAMSON   I don't get it. This is your big idea? One day you say to yourself, before I die, I must figure out the whole pant leg mystery? Then, on to the Colonel's secret recipe!

DR. GUZMAN    I realize it may seem trivial. But what you fail to understand, Mr. Adamson, is that genetics is like real estate. Location location location. It's not the house. It's the neighbourhood. Because you just never know who's going to move in next door.

*Making sure DR. GUZMAN is not looking, MR. ADAMSON throws the book toward the phone on the shelf. He misses, the book falls to the floor.*

*To disguise the noise he sneezes.*

Bless you.

MR. ADAMSON    Bless me?

DR. GUZMAN    It's just an expression.

MR. ADAMSON    People used to believe when you sneeze, you are in that brief moment between Heaven and Hell. And if you were blessed, you'd be saved from damnation.

*MR. ADAMSON tries again with the book. Again he sneezes.*

*This time, THEO sneezes simultaneously.*

DR. GUZMAN    *Noroc.*

## Auditorium

CYNTHIA    Bless you.

THEO    Thank you. In Romania, they say *noroc*. To your luck.

CYNTHIA    I'll have to remember that.

## Laboratory

MR. ADAMSON    A sneeze means someone is talking about you. One sneeze good. Two bad.

> *DR. GUZMAN notices the book on the floor. She grabs it, puts it on a shelf.*

DR. GUZMAN    You know what three means? You're catching a cold.

## Auditorium

> *CYNTHIA writes on the board...*

CYNTHIA    Fibonacci is a recursive sequence, where each number is the sum of the previous two. You start with the numbers zero and one. And you add them together, which gives you the next number, which is one. Then you add the last two numbers together, one and one, and that gives you two. Then again, you add the last two numbers together, one and two, and that gives you three. And so on.

THEO        Okay. So what does that mean?

CYNTHIA     So what's fascinating is that you have been picking your numbers along the Fibonacci sequence.

THEO        I don't understand.

CYNTHIA     Don't you see? The Fibonacci sequence is seen in everything. In science. In nature. In how honeybees multiply. When you cut open a pineapple or a pine cone, they are arranged in a Fibonacci pattern.

            *CYNTHIA draws a spiral on the board.*

            And if you draw arcs from Fibonacci numbers, you end up with a spiral, like in seashells, galaxies, and even in our very own molecules. It's in the architecture of the Acropolis. It's there behind Jesus in Dalí's *Sacrament of the Last Supper.*

THEO        What are you saying, that this Fibonacci has something to do with Jesus?

CYNTHIA     Who the hell knows? But it's everywhere. And Fibonacci gave us *the golden ratio*, which we see in the dimensions of a credit card or a belt buckle or a widescreen TV. The Fibonacci sequence is integral to the structure of the universe and everything in it. It's in our very own DNA.

THEO            But I don't get it. Why am I choosing my coin flips based on these Fibonacci numbers?

CYNTHIA         I was hoping *you* would tell *me*.

THEO            Is that why you're here?

CYNTHIA         I'm here because there's a genetic disease in my family.

## Laboratory

DR. GUZMAN      Of course... I didn't set out on a mission to find the PLO gene. I was going to discover the gene for RP. Retinitis pigmentosa. Cure blindness. Cure myself. That was going to be my life's work.

                *DR. GUZMAN tries using her white cane to pry open the briefcase.*

MR. ADAMSON     That would have been quite a story.

DR. GUZMAN      Damn right. Instant immortality.

                *She whacks the briefcase with her cane.*

                What is this thing made of, osmium diboride?

                *She hurls the white cane across the room.*

                Even the quest was a compelling story. Afflicted researcher strives to identify her own gene before she goes blind. The grant money came pouring in. I even used my own tissue as a genetic sample. Like the guy who discovered the suicide gene. Then killed himself.

MR. ADAMSON   Wow.

DR. GUZMAN   I know. Seems paradoxical, doesn't it? The suicide gene is a dead end, so to speak. It should have been a lethal mutation. Like, say, a gene that caused a target-shaped rash to appear on your forehead right before hunting season.

*MR. ADAMSON picks up the white cane.*

MR. ADAMSON   So how can there be a gene for suicide?

DR. GUZMAN   Ah, but what if the suicide gene gives you some sort of competitive advantage? Maybe people who have this gene are more fearless. They take bigger risks. Have more sex, more progeny. Before they pull the trigger.

MR. ADAMSON   My dad committed suicide.

DR. GUZMAN   If you give me some blood, I can test you for the gene.

MR. ADAMSON   Then what?

DR. GUZMAN   Then you know. That's all. Diagnose, *adios*.

MR. ADAMSON   But if you know the gene, why can't you just cure the disease?

DR. GUZMAN    It's not that easy. For starters, you need a billion dollars to go from gene to drug. *And* you need a lot of luck.

> *Delicately,* MR. *ADAMSON attempts to bring down the phone using the white cane.*

And somebody got lucky. Somebody else.

MR. ADAMSON    Somebody else discovered your gene?

DR. GUZMAN    Using a culture of my own cells. This young kid doing his post-doc throws up a prayer and discovers the very gene I'd spent my whole life chasing.

MR. ADAMSON    That doesn't seem fair.

DR. GUZMAN    Fair? Is it fair that you can't walk? Is it fair that some prick stole my gene from right under my nose? Fairness is not in the equation. Science doesn't belong to anybody. It's not a creation. It's a discovery. If somebody didn't accidentally stumble upon penicillin, the double helix, or the goddamn Slinky, somebody else would have. Can you imagine the world today without a Slinky? Impossible!

MR. ADAMSON    So why did you fail? You were smart enough, hard-working enough. Motivated enough. You know why you failed?

DR. GUZMAN    The same reason I got defective eyeballs. Short straw.

MR. ADAMSON    But why? Why weren't you the lucky one?

>*The phone crashes to the ground.* DR. GUZMAN *grabs it, puts it away.*

DR. GUZMAN  I might ask you the same thing.

MR. ADAMSON  I'm not unlucky.

DR. GUZMAN  Prove it. Heads or tails.

>*No response.*

Then I can't help you.

>MR. ADAMSON *turns his back to* DR. GUZMAN, *shields her view.*

>*He opens a Bible on his lap, drops something onto the open book.*

MR. ADAMSON  Heads.

>DR. GUZMAN *flips the coin. She tries to catch it, but the coin clatters to the floor.*

DR. GUZMAN  Dammit.

>*She drops to her knees, searches for the coin.*

Things that require peripheral vision. Driving a car, pouring a drink, and, apparently, flipping a damn coin.

>*She finds the coin.*

Tails. Unlucky.

MR. ADAMSON    Or… maybe God wanted me to stay. Just like maybe God wanted you to fail.

DR. GUZMAN    Am I being punished? Have I angered the gods?

MR. ADAMSON    God doesn't get angry, but He has His reasons. Maybe He has bigger successes in store for you. Or maybe He thinks you should be remembered as the person who discovered the gene for putting on pants.

DR. GUZMAN    To assume my best work is behind me, Mr. Adamson, would be a mistake. When I die, my contributions will be celebrated.

MR. ADAMSON    Of course. I'm sure your obituary will be front-page news.

DR. GUZMAN    What's that supposed to mean? Is that a threat? Are you threatening me, Mr. Adamson?

MR. ADAMSON    No. I just—

DR. GUZMAN    Why are you here?

MR. ADAMSON    I'm here because you wanted to see me. That's all. Why do you think I'm here?

DR. GUZMAN    Because, despite evidence to the contrary, I'm not convinced you're unlucky. I don't think you're a one-in-five-quintillion guy. I think you cheated your way into my office and I think you're here for a reason.

MR. ADAMSON   What is that reason?

DR. GUZMAN   I think there's a gun in your briefcase and I think you came here to kill me.

## Auditorium

THEO   I knew there was a reason. There always is.

CYNTHIA   My dad had it. His mom had it.

THEO   That's unfortunate.

CYNTHIA   What do you mean, unfortunate? Are you implying my family is unlucky?

THEO   Of course not. I meant it… randomly.

CYNTHIA   Damn right.

THEO   So this disease runs in your family. And you? Are you affected?

CYNTHIA   I always knew I had a fifty-fifty chance of getting the disease. Only I never felt the need to get tested. It usually appears later in life, so I figured either I have it and I'll deal with it or I don't and I won't. No treatment. No cure. So why bother? Diagnose, *adios*.

THEO   But now you're pregnant.

CYNTHIA        Right. That changes everything. Now I can do something about it.

THEO           What do you mean, do something?

CYNTHIA        Does the luckiest man alive have a problem with choice?

THEO           So that's why you're here. Thought a little luck might help you before you get tested?

CYNTHIA        No. I got tested. Two weeks ago.

THEO           And?

CYNTHIA        I'm positive. The laboratory says I have the disease. It's just a matter of time before it starts to affect me.

THEO           That's… unfortunate. I'm not sure how I mean that.

CYNTHIA        Yeah. I'll have to deal with that later. I've got a bigger problem. I had an amnio last week.

THEO           Okay.

CYNTHIA        And I'm having a girl.

THEO           Congratulations.

CYNTHIA        And I just got the results of the genetic testing.

                *CYNTHIA produces an envelope.*

## Laboratory

DR. GUZMAN    That's why you're here.

MR. ADAMSON    Why do I want to kill you?

DR. GUZMAN    Because I'm a stem-cell researcher. We seem to be unpopular in gun-toting circles.

>    *DR. GUZMAN finds a laser pointer.*

>    Why else are you taking my course?

MR. ADAMSON    If you must know, because God wanted me to.

DR. GUZMAN    God wanted you to take my genetics course.

MR. ADAMSON    Yes.

DR. GUZMAN    Why?

MR. ADAMSON    I'm not sure.

DR. GUZMAN    I'm honoured. It's like having the dean recommend your class, only it's *his* boss. Next time you talk to God, ask Him if He'd write me an endorsement on ratemyprofessors.com.

MR. ADAMSON    You ask Him. Next time *you* talk to Him.

| DR. GUZMAN | How, exactly, did He tell you to take my course? Does He come to you in dreams? Do you see patterns in your Rice Krispies? |
|---|---|

| MR. ADAMSON | I ask him questions. He answers. |
|---|---|

| DR. GUZMAN | Like what course should I take? Is this canta-loupe ripe? |
|---|---|

| MR. ADAMSON | I really don't think it's any of your business how I communicate with God. |
|---|---|

| DR. GUZMAN | Maybe it isn't. But you know what? Maybe it is. Why don't you ask Him? |
|---|---|

*DR. GUZMAN finds a magnifying glass.*

| MR. ADAMSON | Ask Him what? |
|---|---|

| DR. GUZMAN | I mean, He did bring you here today, didn't He? Why? |
|---|---|

| MR. ADAMSON | He will tell me when He is ready. |
|---|---|

| DR. GUZMAN | Perhaps He brought you here to answer my questions. So why don't you ask Him if He is, in fact, any of my business. What do you need? Tea leaves? All I have are coffee grounds. I could sprinkle them on the floor. |
|---|---|

| MR. ADAMSON | There's no reason to be disrespectful. I don't mock your beliefs. |
|---|---|

| DR. GUZMAN | I have no beliefs to mock. |
|---|---|

MR. ADAMSON    You believe in science.

DR. GUZMAN    Ha! You could mock my belief in the laws of nature. Make fun of my allegiance to gravity. To the roundness of this planet.

MR. ADAMSON    You're entitled to your beliefs.

DR. GUZMAN    Science is not a belief. It's an absolute.

> DR. GUZMAN *tries using the laser pointer and magnifying glass to melt the lock.*

MR. ADAMSON    I'm not questioning gravity and I'm not disputing the earth is round. But science is not the whole story. It gives us the what, not the why. Why is there gravity? Why is the earth round? Science needs God as much as God needs science.

DR. GUZMAN    Science needs God like an amoeba needs a Golgi apparatus.

> *She laughs at her own joke.*

Why did God want me to fail?

MR. ADAMSON    How should I know?

> *She aims her laser pointer at him.*

DR. GUZMAN    Theorize.

MR. ADAMSON    I don't know. Do you have any blood on your hands?

DR. GUZMAN    Somebody else finding my gene was some kind of punishment?

MR. ADAMSON    It's possible.

DR. GUZMAN    It's absurd.

> *Pause.*

So what does He say?

MR. ADAMSON    Who?

DR. GUZMAN    God. Your creator. Did you ask Him if He is any of my business?

> MR. *ADAMSON shakes his closed fist, lets something drop onto the open Bible in his lap.*

MR. ADAMSON    Yes. For some reason, He said yes.

## Auditorium

THEO    And so?

> CYNTHIA *holds her envelope.*

CYNTHIA    And so I thought I would hedge my bets first. Before I opened it.

THEO    You don't believe in luck. I believe you were quite clear on that.

CYNTHIA    My baby has a fifty per cent chance of inheriting this disease. And the glass is looking half empty right now. So I just thought, if there's anything I could do to fill it up a little bit. Just in case…

THEO    If you don't believe in luck, walk under the ladder.

CYNTHIA    I don't think so.

THEO    Exactly!

CYNTHIA    Well I also avoid stepping in dog poop. Or licking frozen metal. It's called common sense. Don't step in things. Don't lick things. Don't walk *under* things.

THEO    Absolutely nothing to do with bad luck.

CYNTHIA    For God's sake. No, I don't believe in luck, good or bad. I think it's a bunch of bullshit hogwash. It's the mantra of failure. It's the opiate of the atheist masses.

THEO    But?

CYNTHIA    But I believe in Fibonacci.

THEO    And that's why you're here. Because of Fibonacci.

CYNTHIA    Because of my baby. What would you do?

THEO    Tear up the envelope.

CYNTHIA    Don't judge.

THEO    You asked.

CYNTHIA      What I meant to ask, what I'm here to ask is, what, if anything, can I do to optimize things? To change my luck. *Her* luck.

THEO         I heard crossing your fingers sometimes works.

CYNTHIA      Consider them crossed.

THEO         Rabbit's feet. Four-leaf clovers. Sex with lucky men.

CYNTHIA      I'm asking for your help.

THEO         What exactly do you want me to do? Wave a magic wand?

CYNTHIA      Your book is called *Change Your Luck*. I was hoping maybe you would have some insight.

THEO         Really?

CYNTHIA      Desperate times.

THEO         Did you read it?

CYNTHIA      It's bullshit.

*She walks to the shelf, finds the book, flips it open.*

"If you pick the shorter line at the grocery store, cele-brate your good fortune. The more luck you look for, the more you'll find." That's absurd. You're not telling people how to change their luck. Only to recognize it. You won't become luckier, you'll just *feel* luckier.

*She slams the book shut.*

There is absolutely nothing of value in that book. *Change Your Luck*... the whole premise is preposterous.

THEO          So walk under the ladder.

CYNTHIA       It's complete and utter bullshit.

THEO          I got an email from somebody last month. She read my book. The next day she won the lottery.

CYNTHIA       What about the other ten thousand people who read your book and didn't win the lottery?

THEO          Try two million.

CYNTHIA       No shit. Well there are 1,999,999 people out there who deserve a refund. Not to mention a college education.

THEO          These people are trying to improve their lot in life. There's no need to criticize them.

CYNTHIA       I'm criticizing *you*. Your book is a fake.

*CYNTHIA opens the book again.*

"To improve your luck in the dating world, spend more time where single people hang out."

*She stares at THEO, incredulous.*

"In bookstores. In coffee shops." You forgot *Star Trek* conventions!

THEO            What's wrong with that? It's sound advice.

CYNTHIA         Your idea is to improve the odds of random events by increasing the numerator. That's not improving your luck. That's improving your percentages.

THEO            Tomayto tomahto.

CYNTHIA         If I want to improve my odds of winning the lottery, I should buy more lottery tickets? That's your best-selling technique?

THEO            It works.

CYNTHIA         So if I want to improve the odds of having a healthy child, your solution is I should have quintuplets? That doesn't help the little girl I have in my uterus right now, does it? Does it?

THEO            No. It doesn't.

CYNTHIA         You should be ashamed of yourself. You're scamming innocent people.

THEO            I'm giving them hope.

CYNTHIA         You're taking advantage of their desperation. And why? For a few more bucks? Do you really need more money?

THEO            All the money from this book is going to charity.

CYNTHIA       How noble. So why are you doing this?

THEO          I wanted to share my good fortune. That's all.

              *CYNTHIA holds out her envelope.*

CYNTHIA       Then open this envelope.

THEO          Okay. I will.

              *Pause.*

              If you walk under the ladder.

## Laboratory

DR. GUZMAN    Okay. Now we're getting somewhere. What the hell
              is that?

              *MR. ADAMSON holds up a small bone.*

MR. ADAMSON   It's a bone. Technically, a bone fragment.

DR. GUZMAN    Fascinating.

MR. ADAMSON   It's the fragment of bone that severed my spinal cord.
              I started carrying it around as kind of a reminder.

DR. GUZMAN    In case you forgot you were in a wheelchair?

              *DR. GUZMAN climbs the ladder, holding the briefcase.*

MR. ADAMSON    I don't suppose you've heard of *astragali*? Animal knucklebones. The ancient Greeks used them to talk to their gods. Before a big battle they would throw them, and depending on how they landed they would make strategic decisions.

DR. GUZMAN    Making Greece the powerhouse it is today. So you make your decisions by tossing this... vertebra?

MR. ADAMSON    When I need God's guidance. That's how I chose your course.

DR. GUZMAN    It seems I was premature in dismissing "exceptionally stupid."

> DR. GUZMAN *drops the briefcase. It crashes onto the ground. It doesn't open.*

MR. ADAMSON    Can you please not do that?

DR. GUZMAN    Then tell me the combination. I think we can safely eliminate six six six, six six six?

MR. ADAMSON    Here's how I look at it. God decided, for the time being, I would best serve Him from a wheelchair. The instrument which He used to achieve this was this very bone. So by using it in this way, I, myself, have become an instrument of God.

DR. GUZMAN    Hallelujah! Let's open our hymn books and sing "Come Speak to Me, O Lord, With Thy Holy Bone."

MR. ADAMSON    What I don't understand is why He wanted me to talk to you about this.

DR. GUZMAN    Maybe He made a mistake.

MR. ADAMSON    No. He has His reasons. He always does.

DR. GUZMAN    So you decided to take my course because your bone-dice—

MR. ADAMSON    I call it my "instrument."

DR. GUZMAN    Because your bone-dice instrument came up heads.

MR. ADAMSON    *(shows her the bone fragment)* This bone has four faces, like an *astragalus*. So for two-option questions, I call these two sides heads and these two sides tails. When I asked Him about you just now, it came up like this. Heads means yes.

DR. GUZMAN    Do you use this thing to make every decision in your life? "Do you want fries with that, sir?" Hmm, I'm not sure… Excuse me a moment while I confer with my bone-dice.

> DR. GUZMAN *examines the briefcase on the floor. It's intact.*

Since when do they make briefcases an eleven on the Mohs hardness scale?

MR. ADAMSON    I use my instrument for important things. Like taking your exam.

DR. GUZMAN    You used that thing to answer my questions?

MR. ADAMSON    I put it on my desk, rolled it quietly one hundred and fifty times.

DR. GUZMAN    Are you telling me that this bone succeeded in randomly getting every question wrong?

MR. ADAMSON    I didn't say randomly.

DR. GUZMAN    You think God got you a goose egg?

*(into voice recorder)* Subject claims all questions wrong the result of one hundred and fifty flips of magical bone.

MR. ADAMSON    I think it is God's will that we are here, right now, face to face.

DR. GUZMAN    Let say we indulge your hypothesis. Then why? Why, Mr. One-In-Five-Quintillion-Random-Bone-Dice-Guy? Why does He want us here, right now, face to face?

MR. ADAMSON    That's what I've been trying to figure out. But if I hadn't gotten every question wrong on your exam, would you have even let me in the door?

## Auditorium

CYNTHIA    No. I'm not going to play your patronizing games.

THEO    Suit yourself. Doesn't matter, anyway. My luck is not transferable. I have no stake in your result, so no matter what your envelope says, you will walk out the door and my charmed life will go on. My luck, I'm sorry to say, is of no use to you.

CYNTHIA     Open it anyway. What's the harm?

THEO     There's a fifty-fifty chance you'll head straight to some clinic. I don't want blood on my hands.

CYNTHIA     I haven't decided what I'm going to do. Not that it's any of your business.

THEO     If you like, I'd be happy to rip up the envelope.

CYNTHIA     I couldn't do that to her.

        *Pause.*

        You wouldn't understand. You don't have any kids.

THEO     No. I don't.

CYNTHIA     Well, that's… unfortunate.

        *CYNTHIA heads for the door.*

THEO     I lied.

        *Pause.*

        The truth is, you can't change your luck.

## Laboratory

DR. GUZMAN    Perhaps not. But then why did He send you here if it wasn't to kill me?

*DR. GUZMAN finds a glass pipette.*

MR. ADAMSON    It's possible He sent me here to inform you, or even to warn you, that you have ventured into God's territory.

DR. GUZMAN    What exactly is God's territory? The Middle East? The Vatican? Alabama?

MR. ADAMSON    This lab. You're playing around with something sacred. You're trying to rewrite God's very own text. Our genetic code. Why is that fair game? Nobody would dare mess around with Shakespeare, and Shakespeare is merely one of His creations.

DR. GUZMAN    Shakespeare never killed anyone. He never blinded anyone. He never took away someone's child by making a typo.

MR. ADAMSON    God doesn't make typos.

*DR. GUZMAN draws GAG --> GTG.*

DR. GUZMAN    No? Well your God must have been a little hungover one morning because He stuck a thymine instead of an adenine in the hemoglobin gene, so I'm pretty sure He goofed.

MR. ADAMSON     God does not goof.

DR. GUZMAN     Is that right? Did He intend for this one simple poly-morphism to cause the red blood cell to sickle? Did He intend for one in five hundred black people to be crippled by this disease? I'm pretty sure He meant to hit the *A* on his four-key typewriter.

MR. ADAMSON     How do you know that? What if Shakespeare intended to write, "To pee or not to pee." Maybe Hamlet had a prostate problem and *that* was the question. Or why don't we just assume the writer did what he intended to do, and accept it at face value?

DR. GUZMAN     So what did your God intend to do? What was He thinking when He *created* sickle-cell disease? Or muscular dystrophy? Or retinitis pigmentosa?

    *Pause.*

    What was He thinking when He put you in a sex-free wheelchair for the rest of your goddamn life?

MR. ADAMSON     I will walk again. I will have children. When God decides it's time.

DR. GUZMAN     Right. While you sit around and wait for two legs and a penis to drop from the sky, my job is to hit the delete button and fix what needs to be fixed, by whatever means necessary.

MR. ADAMSON     My job is to preserve and protect His original man-uscript. In all its glory.

DR. GUZMAN    How, exactly, do you intend to do that? You can't even preserve and protect your own underpants.

MR. ADAMSON    People think just because you're in a wheelchair, you're an easy target. I *can* protect myself, Dr. Guzman.

> *DR. GUZMAN finds a bottle of clear liquid.*

> *She sets it on top of the briefcase.*

DR. GUZMAN    I don't see how. Unless you're hiding a weapon in here.

## Auditorium

CYNTHIA    So you admit it! You might want to change the title of your book.

THEO    To what? You're completely screwed and there's nothing you can do about it? You think that's what people want to hear?

CYNTHIA    Doesn't matter. You should tell them the truth.

THEO    Fine, here it is. I think you were born unlucky. I think your baby has the misfortune of having an unlucky mother, and if you open that envelope, I'm betting the test is positive. You can't change your luck. You got what you got. I'm sorry.

CYNTHIA     Don't be sorry. There's no reason to apologize for being an arrogant, know-it-all prick. Some people are born that way. You got what you got.

THEO     I *am* sorry. I'd help you if I could.

CYNTHIA     Go to hell.

THEO     I couldn't save my wife. And you expect me to help *you*?

CYNTHIA     What happened to your wife?

THEO     Car accident. A long time ago. Only one of us survived. Guess which one.

CYNTHIA     The lucky one?

THEO     The one who wasn't pregnant.

CYNTHIA     I'm sorry.

THEO     Apparently, my luck has an asterisk.

*CYNTHIA heads for the door.*

This Fibonacci sequence. I don't understand. Why would my bets be following that pattern? That's quite a…

CYNTHIA     Here's what I can't figure out. Why *this* sequence? There are hundreds of mathematical sequences out there. You could have picked your coin flips according to the digits of pi. Why Fibonacci? This sequence you just happened to choose is almost... spiritual.

THEO        I didn't choose it. It chose me.

CYNTHIA     Yeah. That's the thing. I'd feel better if *you* had chosen *it*. It would make the probabilities more palatable.

            *Pause.*

            Theo, why is your briefcase combination the first six digits of the Fibonacci sequence?

THEO        I don't know why. Those numbers just came to me one day.

CYNTHIA     You had no idea about their significance?

THEO        No. I just knew I'd never forget them.

            THEO *checks his watch.*

CYNTHIA     You're a strange man, Theo. Mathematically speaking.

THEO        What did you mean, spiritual? You mean God? Is this God communicating with me?

CYNTHIA     Is God giving you gambling tips? That's your theory?

THEO        It's possible. God invented Las Vegas.

CYNTHIA     God invented religious delusion.

THEO        Well, what's *your* theory? Why am I following this Fibonacci sequence?

CYNTHIA      I don't have a theory. I just identified a pattern. The question is, why? Why are you following this pre-determined pattern? It's almost as if your picks have already been written down and sealed away.

*THEO's phone starts ringing in his briefcase.*

THEO        And I'm just opening the envelopes. One by one.

CYNTHIA      You don't have to. You could just tear it up and walk away right now. You could die a lucky man.

## Laboratory

MR. ADAMSON   Do you really believe I would do that?

DR. GUZMAN     If anyone is an easy target, it is me. A public advocate of stem-cell research. A blind woman alone in a basement lab, foolish enough to open her door in the middle of the night.

*DR. GUZMAN uncorks the bottle.*

MR. ADAMSON   What is that?

DR. GUZMAN     $H_2SO_4$. pH of 1.26. This will burn through anything.

*MR. ADAMSON flips his astragalus.*

MR. ADAMSON    Tails!

DR. GUZMAN    Ah. So you're saying we should increase our sample size? I might make a scientist out of you yet.

> *DR. GUZMAN pulls out her coin, flips it. Again she tries to catch it. Again she misses. The coin falls to the floor.*

Dammit. I could have sworn I was able to flip a goddamn coin six months ago.

> *DR. GUZMAN examines her glasses.*

> *She drops to the floor, searches for the coin.*

Mr. Adamson, are you in favour of embryonic stem-cell research?

MR. ADAMSON    No. But that doesn't mean—

DR. GUZMAN    You, if anyone, should be cheerleading this whole thing. You have the most to gain.

> *She finds the coin, shows MR. ADAMSON.*

Heads, not your lucky day. Do you actually know what the odds are of you ever walking again? One in a billion. That's with a B.

MR. ADAMSON    I'm an optimist.

DR. GUZMAN    You're an idiot. The only chance you have is if some stem-cell researcher gets lucky and stumbles on a cure. Before some myopic fundamentalist kills us all in the name of God. If you want to walk to your altar one day, we are your only hope.

> DR. GUZMAN *draws up the sulphuric acid in a pipette.*

MR. ADAMSON    That doesn't make what you're doing right.

DR. GUZMAN    Oh, so it's a matter of morality, of conscience. Why didn't you say that, instead of invoking your nebulous God construct?

> *She attempts to burn her way into the briefcase.*

MR. ADAMSON    God gives us our conscience.

DR. GUZMAN    Actually, the conscience gene was discovered two years ago. Made quite a splash. Fox News called it "The Cheatin' Gene"! Where the hell did you get this briefcase, Mr. Bond?

MR. ADAMSON    But where did the gene come from in the first place? We are here because God created us.

DR. GUZMAN    Bullshit.

MR. ADAMSON    Prove it.

DR. GUZMAN    Prove what?

MR. ADAMSON    If you're a scientist, prove God doesn't exist.

DR. GUZMAN    That's impossible.

MR. ADAMSON    Exactly.

DR. GUZMAN    But that's the wrong question. Unicorns with paisley headbands may have roamed the planet a million years ago. But they didn't *need* to. The God hypothesis was advanced to fill a void. To explain the inexplicable. So the better question is, can we prove the *need* for God doesn't exist?

MR. ADAMSON    And?

DR. GUZMAN    And I can.

## Auditorium

*The phone continues to ring.*

THEO    I don't think so. That's Vegas on the phone. They want my pick.

CYNTHIA    Fine, go ahead, risk it all. But if *I'm* right, if Fibonacci is right, your next pick should be tails.

THEO    Say it does come up tails. Then what?

CYNTHIA    Then you take a cold shower.

THEO    No, I mean, what if your Fibonacci sequence holds true? What would that mean? That maybe somebody is trying to tell me something? That I have some pretty powerful cosmic forces in my corner?

CYNTHIA  Sure. You're a conduit to the spiritual centre of the universe. God is speaking to you via your coin flips. You do have quite the ego.

*THEO's phone stops ringing.*

I should be going. You have a coin to flip. And a God complex to indulge.

## Laboratory

DR. GUZMAN  God is unnecessary. God is redundant. There is nothing in the universe that cannot be explained by science. We are the product of genes and evolution and probability. We do not need God to be our fudge factor.

*DR. GUZMAN looks in a drawer.*

MR. ADAMSON  So life began purely randomly. In the beginning, there was nothing. And then all of a sudden, one day, without any help from God...

DR. GUZMAN  Or aliens.

MR. ADAMSON  All of a sudden, life appears.

DR. GUZMAN  Plausible.

MR. ADAMSON  Far-fetched.

DR. GUZMAN    Of course. But far less far-fetched than postulating divine intervention.

MR. ADAMSON    So life magically appears one day...

DR. GUZMAN    Not magically. First there was the Big Bang. Or does His existence preclude the Big Bang?

MR. ADAMSON    Not if He was the Big Banger.

DR. GUZMAN    Well, unfortunately, since He hadn't yet created plasma TV, or actual plasma for that matter, we'll never know for sure what actually happened at the moment of the Big Bang. Everyone has their own theory.

> *DR. GUZMAN finds a Bunsen burner.*

Let's see how your 007 briefcase likes a thousand degrees Celsius.

MR. ADAMSON    Heads!

DR. GUZMAN    N equals three? Why not? Let there be heads.

> *DR. GUZMAN flips another coin. This time she doesn't even try to catch it. She doesn't bother looking for it.*

> *MR. ADAMSON searches for the coin.*

But we do have a supercollider that can approximate the condition of the universe one billionth of a second *after* the Big Bang, which gave us the Higgs boson, your "God particle," followed by the main attraction, our entire universe.

MR. ADAMSON    But not life.

*MR. ADAMSON locates the coin.*

It's tails.

DR. GUZMAN    But everything necessary for life. First came our sun. Then came the earth and its big primordial soup, the prebiotic oceans, from which the first self-replicating DNA was born.

MR. ADAMSON    Spontaneously. Randomly. Miraculously.

DR. GUZMAN    Yes. Yes. And hell no!

*DR. GUZMAN finds a flint lighter.*

MR. ADAMSON    So life began on Earth at the exact time and place when conditions could support life. Our sun happened to be the perfect age. Our planet happened to be the perfect temperature. Then, out of this soup, life just began. What are the chances of that?

DR. GUZMAN    One in ten to the fortieth. About the same chance as a monkey sitting down at a keyboard and randomly typing a passage from Shakespeare.

MR. ADAMSON    Doesn't that seem far-fetched to you?

DR. GUZMAN    Sure. Unless.

MR. ADAMSON   Unless what?

DR. GUZMAN   Unless that monkey who sat down at a keyboard was exceptionally *lucky*, and just happened to type *Hamlet* on its very first try.

> *DR. GUZMAN tries to light the Bunsen burner.*

Mr. Adamson, are you sure you don't believe in luck?

## Auditorium

THEO   Being lucky is not all it's cracked up to be. Doesn't necessarily mean you're better off. Or happier.

CYNTHIA   Poor rich baby. Money can't buy you happiness? Should we write a country song?

THEO   Forget I said anything.

CYNTHIA   In psych class, we read that lottery winners got an immediate jump in their happiness scores, but a few months later they returned back to their baseline.

THEO   So you can't change your happiness *or* your luck.

CYNTHIA   Not true. Rich people *are* happier, but only if they earn the money themselves. Stolen loot, lotteries… not so much.

THEO   Why is that?

CYNTHIA        Because it's cheating. And they feel guilty. Do you feel guilty?

THEO           Should I?

CYNTHIA        Did you know people who won the lottery with numbers they chose themselves end up happier than those who won with randomly selected numbers?

THEO           Because they think they deserve it.

CYNTHIA        Idiots.

THEO           Happy idiots.

CYNTHIA        Have you earned your wealth? Do you deserve it?

THEO           Not a penny.

CYNTHIA        There you go.

THEO           Maybe that's why I get death threats every day.

CYNTHIA        From who?

THEO           People who don't think I deserve my good fortune.

CYNTHIA        People who think you're cheating.

THEO           How do I prove I'm not?

CYNTHIA        By losing?

THEO           What if I can't lose?

CYNTHIA     Have you tried?

THEO        How exactly do you *try* to lose a coin flip?

CYNTHIA     Right. I see your point. But if you could. Would you?

            *Pause.*

            Theo, do you *want* to lose?

THEO        *What I want...* doesn't matter, does it?

CYNTHIA     If only you could perform a luck-ectomy.

THEO        If only.

CYNTHIA     How would one go about doing that? Carry a black
            cat under a ladder on Friday the thirteenth?

            *From a hidden compartment in his briefcase* THEO
            *pulls out a gun.*

THEO        Or maybe I could use this.


## Laboratory


DR. GUZMAN   I'm starting to think there's nothing in here.

             *DR. GUZMAN cannot get the Bunsen burner to light.
             She keeps trying.*

MR. ADAMSON  Then can I have it back?

DR. GUZMAN   Perhaps we could work out a trade of some kind. Is there something *you* have that *I* might want?

MR. ADAMSON   Like what?

DR. GUZMAN   I always thought luck was a bunch of bullshit hogwash. But after enough near misses and why me's, you start to consider other hypotheses. What if I told you there are instances where somebody won the lottery, and then their child also won?

MR. ADAMSON   I would say they are blessed.

DR. GUZMAN   Dammit, think like a scientist. In a population of thousands of lottery winners, what are the chances, based on randomness alone, that there will be families with multiple winners?

> MR. *ADAMSON points at the board, at the previously written 13%.*

MR. ADAMSON   Um… Thirteen per cent?

DR. GUZMAN   Here's the funny thing. The numbers are greater than they should be. Families are winning lotteries *disproportionately*. And how do you explain the family in Norway where a woman won the lottery. Then her father won. And then her son.

MR. ADAMSON   They're a bunch of cheaters?

DR. GUZMAN   They were investigated. And paid in full. Any other ideas?

MR. ADAMSON   Really good cheaters?

DR. GUZMAN   Did you notice the pattern? Grandfather. Daughter. Grandson.

This is the same pattern as the pant-leg gene. X-linked.

*She draws an X on the board.*

MR. ADAMSON   What are you saying, luck is genetic?

DR. GUZMAN   I'm asking the question.

## Auditorium

CYNTHIA   What the hell?

THEO   Protection. I've carried it with me since I was fourteen. I used to be an easy target.

CYNTHIA   Put it away.

THEO   Relax. It's not loaded. Fully.

CYNTHIA   What do you mean, fully?

THEO   Ever heard of Russian roulette?

*THEO spins the cylinder.*

CYNTHIA   It's been nice talking to you.

*CYNTHIA walks toward the door.*

THEO            Doesn't seem fair though, does it? I should really use three bullets, not one? To be fair.

CYNTHIA         How long have you been suicidal?

THEO            If I wanted to commit suicide, I'd put all six bullets in.

CYNTHIA         And that would end your lucky streak once and for all, wouldn't it? This time, you won't give them a choice.

THEO            Well I've been wondering… maybe I should test my luck. What do you think?

CYNTHIA         I think you need to see a shrink.

THEO            Saw one. "Depressive Disorder. Schizoid tendencies. Excessive and inappropriate guilt." He recommended medication.

CYNTHIA         Exactly.

THEO            Then he asked me for my Final Four picks.

*THEO puts the gun in his pocket.*

                Turns out, when it comes to actually pulling the trigger, I'm a chicken. I think I was born that way.

## Laboratory

DR. GUZMAN    What if people are born lucky? Or unlucky? Some families are tall. Some have blue eyes. And some families you'd swear have horseshoes up their ass. How else do you explain the Bush presidencies?

MR. ADAMSON   How is that even possible? I mean, I see how a genetic defect can give you a disease. But how could this work with luck?

DR. GUZMAN    In order to answer that, you'd have to understand the molecular basis of luck.

MR. ADAMSON   Which is?

DR. GUZMAN    Damned if I know.

*She gives up on the Bunsen burner, throws the lighter across the room.*

But that doesn't mean I can't hypothesize. Let's say you have a gene that makes you smell bad. You lack an enzyme. Upshot is, you stink.

MR. ADAMSON   I stink?

DR. GUZMAN    So you go through life smelly. Girls don't like you. Teachers don't like you. You can't get a job. Maybe you step in front of a car, end up in a wheelchair. But you know what? You don't even know you smell. And you think you're just one incredibly unlucky guy.

MR. ADAMSON   You're saying if I go to Vegas and put twenty bucks on black, there's something in my genes that causes the ball to land on red?

DR. GUZMAN   Or... something makes you pick black in the first place. When you should have picked—

MR. ADAMSON   Heads!

*DR. GUZMAN gives a coin to MR. ADAMSON.*

DR. GUZMAN   What is luck anyway? What if it's just precognition? What if you woke up this morning and you already knew what was going to happen today?

MR. ADAMSON   I'd probably roll on past your office.

DR. GUZMAN   And go straight to the corner store to buy a lottery ticket. Wouldn't you?

MR. ADAMSON   I might.

*MR. ADAMSON flips the coin, smacks it on the back of his hand.*

DR. GUZMAN   And you'd win. Because you already knew the outcome. Of everything. And you'd become one very rich man.

MR. ADAMSON   Tails.

*MR. ADAMSON looks to the heavens in frustration.*

DR. GUZMAN   But if nobody knew you could see the future, if nobody knew your secret, the world would just think you were one very lucky guy.

## Auditorium

CYNTHIA   Were you born lucky? Were you a lucky child?

THEO   I wouldn't say that. Missed a lot of school. I was kind of a loner. My best friends were probably Ernie and Bert.

CYNTHIA   You mean Bert and Ernie. Who says Ernie and Bert?

THEO   Lots of people, check it out.

CYNTHIA   I will. Were your parents lucky?

THEO   My dad committed suicide when I was three.

CYNTHIA   So where did *your* luck come from?

THEO   It remains a mystery. Nobody can figure it out. Turns out I'm a normal guy. With a big schlong.

*THEO's phone rings.*

And a lucky streak that refuses to die.

*THEO produces a coin.*

Until now.

*He flips it high in the air. Just as he's about to catch it, CYNTHIA reaches out. She catches the coin, inverts it onto the back of her hand. She and THEO lean in close.*

## Laboratory

MR. ADAMSON    How can you know what's going to happen?

DR. GUZMAN    We already know time is malleable. Maybe there is some molecular basis that lets us modulate a sequence of events.

MR. ADAMSON    But you just said order is everything.

DR. GUZMAN    Yes, but sequences can mutate. And Einstein said time has relativity. So what happens in a certain sequence through one person's eyes might happen in an alternate sequence for a different observer. And what if this warped chronology gives you a priori knowledge? And that's why the "lucky" person chooses red.

MR. ADAMSON    Maybe it's just intuition. A hunch.

DR. GUZMAN    But what is intuition? When someone flips a coin, what is that little voice in your head that says, choose tails. Is that your God or your Devil? Or is it déjà vu? Perhaps some people are born with the ability to see things differently. In a different sequence. And maybe *that's* the gene that you, that *we*, lack.

MR. ADAMSON    Well good luck finding that gene.

DR. GUZMAN     Actually, I think I found it. I happened to stumble upon its next-door neighbour.

## Auditorium

CYNTHIA    No way! Thank God.

THEO       Thank God? For heads?

CYNTHIA    I knew it. Fibonacci Schmibonacci. Your guesses are completely random. Fibonacci was just...

THEO       A coincidence?

CYNTHIA    It was inevitable. Sooner or later you were bound to diverge. People don't just randomly roll mathematical sequences. It caught up with you. On the twenty-first time. Finally.

THEO       You're pretty happy about that.

CYNTHIA    Well, I was starting to wonder. I mean, what if it came up tails? What would this mean? That all of your picks have come from... somewhere else?

THEO       From God?

CYNTHIA    Who the hell knows? Turns out your picks came from nowhere. There was no predetermination. No spiritual or scientific questions to be pondered. Just a coin flip gone bad.

*Pause.*

You seem disappointed.

THEO          A little. I was kind of hoping it would come up tails.

CYNTHIA       You're sad because there is no spiritual reason for your lucky streak? You're not God's chosen one? You're just a statistical aberration?

THEO          Thanks. I feel a lot better now.

*The phone starts to ring in the briefcase.*

CYNTHIA       Sorry to disappoint you. But math is absolute. You can't mess with it. Sooner or later, probability will prevail.

*CYNTHIA finds her autographed book, prepares to leave.*

*THEO snaps open the briefcase, reaches for his phone.*

THEO          I liked it better when I was an instrument of God.

## Laboratory

MR. ADAMSON   You're joking, right? You can't expect me to believe—

DR. GUZMAN   I understand your skepticism. I know it sounds implausible. There's a reason nobody in the department knows I'm working on this.

MR. ADAMSON   How exactly does somebody find the gene for luck?

DR. GUZMAN   I started with those lucky families. I played a hunch and discovered all the winners put on their pants left leg first. Then I analyzed their DNA and incorporated gene candidates into mice. And I went looking for the luckiest mouse.

MR. ADAMSON   How can you tell a lucky mouse from an unlucky mouse? The one with the most cheese?

DR. GUZMAN   Exactly! Now you're thinking like a scientist! I simply designed a random reward generator and identified the mouse with the most cheese.

MR. ADAMSON   Then you killed it?

DR. GUZMAN   Wouldn't you know, just as I was about to euthanize him, the phone rang and the lucky bastard got away.

MR. ADAMSON   Really?

DR. GUZMAN   No. I killed him! If some higher power wants you dead, you're dead, right? But I think I found it. On the X chromosome. Right next door to the PLO gene.

MR. ADAMSON   You've found the gene for luck?

DR. GUZMAN   First I need more data, or I will be discredited and put out to pasture for good. I don't have much time left. I need to find a control… an exceptionally unlucky human being.

## Auditorium

*THEO speaks into the phone.*

THEO   It's me. Put everything on tails.

*CYNTHIA gasps, drops her book.*

## Laboratory

DR. GUZMAN   It's easy to find lucky people. But how do you find the unlucky ones? The unluckiest of them die. Usually in freak accidents, like playing with loaded guns.

*DR. GUZMAN rummages through a drawer. MR. ADAMSON moves closer.*

MR. ADAMSON   So you need to get lucky to find an unlucky person to validate your luck gene? That's a bit ironic.

DR. GUZMAN       Irony is like luck. Not everybody who thinks they
                 got it got it.

MR. ADAMSON      I'll have to remember that.

> MR. ADAMSON *steals the door key from her lab-coat
> pocket.*

DR. GUZMAN       It seems you *do* have something I want, Mr.
                 Adamson.

> DR. GUZMAN *produces a tourniquet.*

                 Your blood.

## Auditorium

CYNTHIA          What the hell? Your coin said heads.

THEO             Call it a hunch.

CYNTHIA          A hunch? How much money did you bet?

THEO             All of it. Eight hundred and fifty million. Give
                 or take.

CYNTHIA          Holy shit. Eight hundred and fifty million dollars.
                 On tails. On a hunch. How could you bet against
                 your lucky coin flip?

THEO             How could I bet against Fibonacci?

## Laboratory

MR. ADAMSON    I couldn't do that.

DR. GUZMAN    Your DNA would be most useful for my research.

MR. ADAMSON    That's why you wanted to see me. You needed me for your research.

DR. GUZMAN    First I needed to establish if you were, in fact, luck deficient. Or if you were cheating. I think I have my answer.

MR. ADAMSON    Right. Yes, I'm starting to understand.

DR. GUZMAN    I'm not asking you to believe the science. I probably wouldn't myself. I'm just asking you for some blood.

MR. ADAMSON    Have you even thought about the implications of what you're doing? I mean, what if, God forbid, you're right?

DR. GUZMAN    Did you know that Nobel Prize winners live two years longer than nominees?

MR. ADAMSON    Dr. Guzman, who wants an unlucky child?

## Auditorium

CYNTHIA     I wouldn't. I'd just take the money and run.

THEO        Run where? Do what?

CYNTHIA     How much does it cost to cure a genetic disease?

THEO        When I die, all my money is being left to medical research.

CYNTHIA     Really?

THEO        Eye research.

CYNTHIA     Why eye research?

THEO        I knew someone.

CYNTHIA     I'm going blind.

THEO        What do you mean?

CYNTHIA     Retinitis pigmentosa. RP. You lose your peripheral vision.

THEO        That's your genetic disease? RP?

CYNTHIA     Yes. That's quite a…

THEO        Coincidence?

CYNTHIA       I need to open the envelope.

THEO          No. You don't.

CYNTHIA       I'll be legally blind by the time I'm forty. How can
              I let that happen to my daughter? Knowingly.

THEO          Did *your* mom know you had the gene? Did she know
              you were going to go blind one day?

CYNTHIA       No.

THEO          What if she did? What if she had an envelope, just
              like yours, and she had opened it? What would she
              have done?

CYNTHIA       That's not a fair question.

THEO          I'll tell you what she *should* have done. She should
              have torn up that envelope. Because if she had
              opened it, you wouldn't be here today...

              *The phone rings.*

              And I would have chosen heads. When I should have
              chosen...

              *THEO answers his phone.*

## Laboratory

MR. ADAMSON    Nobody. Nobody wants an unlucky child. People kill innocent babies for lots of reasons. Now you want to add bad luck to that list?

DR. GUZMAN    I'm just trying to help people who are less fortunate. Like you.

MR. ADAMSON    I am not less fortunate.

*MR. ADAMSON moves toward the door.*

DR. GUZMAN    Oh but you are. You have lost the ability to walk. This is not an advantageous adaptation. It's a lethal mutation.

*She writes on the board: LETHAL*

You have returned to that primordial ocean. You will not procreate. Your genes stop here. You are the *definition* of less fortunate. Have we not proven that to your satisfaction?

*DR. GUZMAN grabs a fistful of coins from her beaker.*

Heads or tails, Mr. Adamson? If you get just one coin right, I'll let you go. But if you don't…

MR. ADAMSON    You get my blood.

DR. GUZMAN    What do you say?

*MR. ADAMSON moves to the door. He stops, thinks. He flips his astragalus.*

MR. ADAMSON   It says tails.

DR. GUZMAN   But what do *you* say?

*MR. ADAMSON takes a long look at the door, at the key hidden in his hand, at his astragalus. He spins to face DR. GUZMAN.*

MR. ADAMSON   I say...

*DR. GUZMAN throws her fistful of coins into the air.*

MR. ADAMSON
& THEO   Tails.

*The coins crash to the floor.*

## Auditorium

*THEO hangs up the phone slowly.*

THEO   It was tails.

CYNTHIA   Are you telling me you just won 1.7 *billion* dollars?

THEO   Fibonacci was right.

CYNTHIA   Fibonacci was right.

THEO            What does this mean?

> *THEO and CYNTHIA stare at the board.*

CYNTHIA         It means you can't lose.

## Laboratory

DR. GUZMAN      You can't win, as they say, if you don't play.

> *MR. ADAMSON moves around the room in a tight-
> ening spiral. He checks each coin on the ground.
> DR. GUZMAN slides in behind him, pushes his
> wheelchair.*

So we all play. Even you, Mr. Adamson. Only money
can't buy you a couple of new legs. That's the lottery
you're really playing? That's what you covet.

MR. ADAMSON     If it's God's will.

DR. GUZMAN      Well, you've got to be a little lucky to win, don't you?
Maybe I can help.

MR. ADAMSON     I don't need your help. I'm betting on God.

> *MR. ADAMSON climbs desperately out of the wheel-
> chair, falls to the floor.*
>
> *Frantically, he checks each coin on the ground.*

DR. GUZMAN    That was Pascal's Wager. He said even though the existence of God cannot be determined, we should wager as though God exists. Because that way you have everything to gain and nothing to lose.

MR. ADAMSON    Exactly.

DR. GUZMAN    Only Pascal went *mad*. Mr. Adamson, you're not in a wheelchair because of some divine plan. You were just at the wrong place at the wrong time.

MR. ADAMSON    No! That's not what happened.

DR. GUZMAN    Your bone-dice is nothing but a meaningless coin flip. God has no plans for you because he doesn't exist.

MR. ADAMSON    How do you know that?

DR. GUZMAN    Because luck is embedded in our DNA. So we don't need to invoke anything from above or from beyond. How did life begin? God? Or luck. You don't need both. They're mutually exclusive. It's the chicken *or* the egg. So which is it? Decide for yourself. I say, in the beginning, *in our blood*, there was luck.

> MR. *ADAMSON* slumps against his wheelchair, still on the floor.

MR. ADAMSON    Not a single tails.

DR. GUZMAN    What are the odds?

> MR. *ADAMSON* rolls up his sleeve.

MR. ADAMSON    If I give you my blood, will you give me back my
briefcase?

*DR. GUZMAN produces a syringe and tourniquet.*

DR. GUZMAN    Not only that. I will, one day, repair your defective
gene. I will make you walk again.

*She ties the tourniquet.*

If I'm right, you will become the luckiest man alive.

*DR. GUZMAN jabs the needle into his arm.*

## Auditorium

CYNTHIA    You really can't lose.

THEO    What if… I get a stake in your test?

*THEO produces the gun. He loads it.*

What if this time, I use *six* bullets?

## Laboratory

DR. GUZMAN    Quick and painless.

*She snaps off the tourniquet.*

Thank you, Mr. Adamson.

> *DR. GUZMAN pulls his ID card from her pocket. She glances at it, returns it.*

Theodore. Gift of God.

MR. ADAMSON    How did you know that?

DR. GUZMAN    I had a goldfish named Theodore.

## Auditorium

CYNTHIA    Theo. Please just—

THEO    Open the envelope. Open it.

> *THEO lifts the gun to his head.*

## Laboratory

> *DR. GUZMAN hands MR. ADAMSON his briefcase.*

DR. GUZMAN    I have to know. What's the combination?

MR. ADAMSON    One one two, three five eight.

DR. GUZMAN    Really? Why that number?

> *MR. ADAMSON shows her his watch.*

DR. GUZMAN       11:23:58.

MR. ADAMSON     My watch stopped at the moment of impact.

## Auditorium

CYNTHIA         What the hell—

THEO            If the test result is positive, I'll pull the trigger.

CYNTHIA         Are you insane? Put the gun down.

THEO            Open it. Please. This is what you wanted.

## Laboratory

MR. ADAMSON     What if God doesn't want us to be lucky? What if
                God doesn't want us to win the lottery?

                *DR. GUZMAN moves toward the door.*

DR. GUZMAN      Then that's not *fair*. And maybe we, the terminally
                unfortunate, need to take matters into our own
                hands.

                *DR. GUZMAN feels in her pocket for the key. It's not
                there. She turns.*

                *MR. ADAMSON snaps open the briefcase.*

MR. ADAMSON     Then this is God's will.

*He points a gun at* DR. GUZMAN.

## Auditorium

CYNTHIA     No. Put the gun down. Please.

THEO     I finally figured out how to share my luck. By giving myself a stake in your daughter. I can change your luck.

CYNTHIA     Because you can't lose? Because you're too lucky to die?

THEO     Exactly! So the test result will have to be negative. If I can't lose, she can't lose.

CYNTHIA     You're very kind. And a little psychotic.

THEO     I couldn't help my child. Let me help yours.

CYNTHIA     I'm going to tear it up.

THEO     I'm not going to die. Trust me.

CYNTHIA     How do you know that?

THEO     Because you're here. Something brought you here today. Tell me this. Did you cheat? In the book draw? Are you here, right now, because you stuffed the jar with your name?

## Laboratory

DR. GUZMAN        No. It's not God's will. It's yours.

MR. ADAMSON       This is why He brought me here. This is why He kept
                  me here. I know that now.

## Auditorium

CYNTHIA           No. I didn't cheat. Did *you*? Did you choose me
                  because of my miniskirt?

THEO              No. I swear it was a random draw.

## Laboratory

DR. GUZMAN        *Random dice* brought you here.

MR. ADAMSON       *God* brought me here!

## Auditorium

THEO              *Fibonacci* brought you here. To me. So I can help
                  you. Why else are we both here?

CYNTHIA           Coincidence?

## Laboratory

DR. GUZMAN   Really? He brought you here today to shoot me in cold blood?

MR. ADAMSON   To stop you, one way or another. There *was* a reason. For everything. I was at the *right* place at the *right* time.

## Auditorium

THEO   Are you sure? Let's find out. Open the envelope.

CYNTHIA   You're crazy. You have a fifty-fifty chance of killing yourself.

THEO   I don't believe that. Do you?

## Laboratory

DR. GUZMAN   Why don't we ask Him. Did you, God Almighty, send this man here to kill me? Yes or no.

MR. ADAMSON   I already know the answer, Dr. Guzman.

DR. GUZMAN   Cynthia. My friends call me Cynthia.

MR. ADAMSON   That's… my dog's name.

## Auditorium

CYNTHIA     I don't give a shit what you believe. Do you really
            want to put your life in the hands of a coin flip?

## Laboratory

DR. GUZMAN  Do it. Flip that bone thing. Heads you shoot me,
            in the name of God, and spend the rest of your life
            in a wheelchair praying for a miracle. Tails, you put
            the gun down and I will change your luck. It can be
            our little secret.

            *Pause.*

            Theodore. Theo. One in a billion is nothing if you
            have luck on your side.

## Auditorium

THEO        I am not going to die. Deep down, you know that.
            Trust the numbers. Trust Fibonacci.

## Laboratory

DR. GUZMAN    Trust your instrument. Heads is God. Tails is Science.

MR. ADAMSON   Why tails?

DR. GUZMAN    Call it a hunch. I feel lucky. Today's my birthday.

## Auditorium

CYNTHIA    I don't believe in luck.

THEO    Prove it.

> *THEO drags the ladder in front of CYNTHIA.*

Did you pray for a healthy child?

CYNTHIA    Yes.

THEO    What if I am the answer to your prayers?

> *CYNTHIA pauses, then takes a single step.*

> *CYNTHIA now stands directly under the ladder. She looks up.*

## Auditorium/Laboratory

MR. ADAMSON    Forgive me.

> *MR. ADAMSON points his gun at DR. GUZMAN.*

THEO    Open it.

> *DR. GUZMAN kneels down.*

DR. GUZMAN    Maybe the chicken came first.

> *CYNTHIA holds the envelope.*
>
> *As if she's going to open it.*
>
> *As if she's going to tear it in two.*
>
> *Slowly, simultaneously...*
>
> *...DR. GUZMAN brings her hands together and prays.*
>
> *...THEO raises his gun to his head.*
>
> *...CYNTHIA tears opens the envelope.*
>
> *...MR. ADAMSON shakes his bone-dice. He keeps shaking it.*
>
> *With his gun against his forehead, THEO stares at CYNTHIA.*

*With his gun pointed at* DR. GUZMAN, MR. ADAMSON
*looks down at his Bible.*

*MR. ADAMSON is across from* THEO.

*DR. GUZMAN is across from* CYNTHIA.

*Together, they resemble a double helix of* DNA.

*The board is a mess of diagrams, numbers, and
words, identical to how it appeared in the opening
scene.*

*Simultaneously…*

*…*CYNTHIA *opens the lab report. She looks at* THEO.

*…*MR. ADAMSON *lets his bone-dice drop. He looks
at* DR. GUZMAN.

*Darkness.*

*A single gunshot creates a Big Bang!*

*A sonic boom reverberates through time and space.
Sounds and images of cosmic and microscopic events.
A mirror unbreaks. Time warps before our eyes.*

*Lights up.*

*The wall mirror is now unbroken.*

*The board and the stage now look exactly the same
as they did at the beginning.*

*The opening scene is now recreated.*

*DR. GUZMAN and THEO enter. THEO carries an unopened umbrella.*

*They converge at the whiteboard. It shows a mess of diagrams, numbers, and words.*

*DR. GUZMAN turns to face the board. She finds an eraser, wipes the board clean.*

*THEO turns to face the audience. With mock trepidation, he pops open the umbrella.*

*Playfully, he peers out from under it, looks upward. He closes the umbrella.*

*THEO moves to the ladder. He circles it. Mysteriously. Mischievously.*

*DR. GUZMAN takes a moment to find a marker. She accidentally drops it, picks it up again.*

*Abruptly, THEO ducks under the ladder. He emerges, welcomes the applause.*

*Chest pain! Is he having a heart attack? No, he's just joking around.*

*DR. GUZMAN writes on the board with her left hand: WHICH CAME FIRST?*

*THEO strides to a wall mirror. He stumbles, almost trips on the way.*

*DR. GUZMAN addresses the audience.*

*THEO fixes his hair in the mirror.*

DR. GUZMAN     The question is, which came first?

*THEO suddenly takes a big swing with his umbrella handle, smashing the mirror.*

*end of play*

## End Notes

*Casting*: There should be sufficient similarity between the male actors, such that it is conceivable Mr. Adamson could grow up to be Theo. Similarly, Cynthia could possibly be a younger version of Dr. Guzman.

*Epilogue*: For the bookend closing scene (immediately after the "Big Bang" scene), the director may choose to reverse roles. The actors playing Cynthia and Mr. Adamson may, for this scene, assume the roles (and costumes) of Dr. Guzman and Theo, respectively. In every other way, this scene would be identical to the opening of the play. This reversal was performed successfully for the US premiere production.

*Whiteboard*: As written, the board begins with a "random mess of diagrams, numbers, and words." However, there is an opportunity to use the board in a more specific manner to underscore the theme of the play.

For example, an apparently seamless four-panelled white board may be used. When the play opens, the words "The Big Bang" are seen spanning the entire board (e.g., diagram 1). As the play develops, the characters illustrate their dialogue with the specific drawings denoted in the script. The diagrams, words, and numbers should appear to be haphazardly sketched; however, each drawing is created and positioned precisely as per the diagrams.

Near the end of the play, just prior to the "Big Bang" moment, the board appears to be simply a random mess (e.g., diagram 2). However, immediately after the "Big Bang" and before the epilogue begins, the panels of the whiteboard rearrange their sequence. The audience now sees that "The Big Bang" has been written, once again, across the entire board (e.g., diagram 3).

That is, by *re-sequencing* the boards, the opening scene has now been recreated exactly. This technique was used successfully in the world premiere production.

# THE BIG BANG!

(diagram 1)

G BA -15₀ | WHICH CAME FIRST? | 13% 1 2 3 5 8 | GAG GTG6 6 LUCK GOD | T H T T H H LUCK T T

(diagram 2)

T
THTT T TT WHICH CAME FIRST? $13^o/_o$ $_{1 \ 2 \ 3 \ 5 \ 8}$ G BA $_{-150}$ G A G G T G 6 LUCK GOD

(diagram 3)

## Additional Reading

For those interested in reading more about the topics discussed in the play, you may wish to read:

"Does God Play Dice?" Stephen Hawking's 1999 lecture. The full transcript can be found at: http://www.hawking.org.uk/does-god-play-dice.html.

*The Drunkard's Walk: How Randomness Rules Our Lives* by Leonard Mlodinow.

## Acknowledgements

To have crossed paths with you, I feel:

    A. Lucky
    B. Blessed
    C. All of the above

Thank you so much…

Mandy Bayrami
Ken Cameron
Adam Carpenter
Ellen Close
Joel Cochrane
Richard Cowden
Lee Cromwell
Ian Currie
Trina Davies

Brian Dooley
Jennie Franks
Anton de Groot
Paul Distefano
Annie Gibson
Tuled Giovanazzi
Jit and Cindy Gohill
Jessica Goldman
Braden Griffiths
Terry Gunvordahl
Taryn Haley
Alana Hawley
Louis B. Hobson
Stephen Hunt
Karen Johnson-Diamond
Nancy Kawalek
Kathi Kerbes
Michelle Kneale
David Krebes
Prem and Shamma Lakra
Laura Lottes
Corey Marr
Peter Moller
Simon Mallett
Kevin McKendrick
Colleen Murphy
Rich Orloff
Mieko Ouchi
Gordon Pengilly
Michael Petrasek
Sharon Pollock
Brian Quirt
Chad Rabinovitz
Trevor Rueger

Caroline Russell-King
Kelsey ter Kuile
Jenna Shummoogum
David Sheehan
Everybody Soin
Blake Sproule
Vicki Stroich
Sasha Sullivan
Wes Sutherland
Vern Thiessen
Margaret Whittum

and, especially,

Roopa, Taro, and Siya.

I am grateful for the support and encouragement of:

Alberta Playwrights' Network (Trevor Rueger, Executive Director)

Bloomington Playwrights Project (Chad Rabinovitz, Producing Artistic Director)

Downstage (Simon Mallett, Artistic Director, Ellen Close, Artistic Producer)

Hit & Myth Productions (Joel Cochrane, Artistic Producer)

STAGE (Scientists, Technologists, and Artists Generating Exploration) at the University of California Santa Barbara's NanoSystems Institute (Nancy Kawalek, Founder/Director)

Telluride Playwrights Festival (Jennie Franks, Artistic Director)

Arun Lakra is a writer, doctor, and father. Arun has written a book on laser eye surgery, a supernatural thriller screenplay, a song to protest the demotion of Pluto, a heartfelt ballad about puke, a line of misunderstood T-shirts, and his share of illegible prescriptions. *Sequence* is his second stage play. His first play received rave reviews for balancing a wobbly table in his basement. Arun lives in Calgary with his wife and kids and divides his work week between his creative endeavours and his ophthalmology practice. You can find out more at www.arunlakra.com.

First edition: March 2014
Printed and bound in Canada by Imprimerie Gauvin, Gatineau

Cover design and illustration and diagrams by Jeff Kulak
Book design by Blake Sproule

**PLAYWRIGHTS
CANADA PRESS**

202-269 Richmond St. W.
Toronto, ON
M5V 1X1

416.703.0013
info@playwrightscanada.com
www.playwrightscanada.com

MIX
Paper from
responsible sources
FSC
www.fsc.org    FSC® C100212